T5-CVC-293

COME ALONG TO VIETNAM

COME ALONG TO
VIETNAM

By

JOHN D. KOTULA

WITHDRAWN

Publishers

T. S. DENISON & COMPANY, INC.
Minneapolis

ROCKFORD PUBLIC LIBRARY

T. S. DENISON & COMPANY, INC.

All rights reserved, including the right to reproduce this book, or portions thereof, except that permission is hereby granted to reviewers to quote brief passages in a review to be printed in magazines and newspapers, or for radio and television reviews.

Standard Book Number: 513-01247-8
Library of Congress Card Number: 72-77207
Printed in the United States of America
by The Brings Press
Copyright © MCMLXXIII by T. S. Denison & Co., Inc.
Minneapolis, Minn. 55437

ROCKTON CENTRE

705746   FEB 2 4 1976

J915.97
KOT

DEDICATION

This book is dedicated to Chester A. Richardson, Provincial Senior Advisor, the men who served under him on Advisory Team 37, and the many Vietnamese friends who made my two years in Vietnam a truly memorable experience.

It is also dedicated to my wife Marcy and our children whose patience and understanding made my participation possible.

CONTENTS

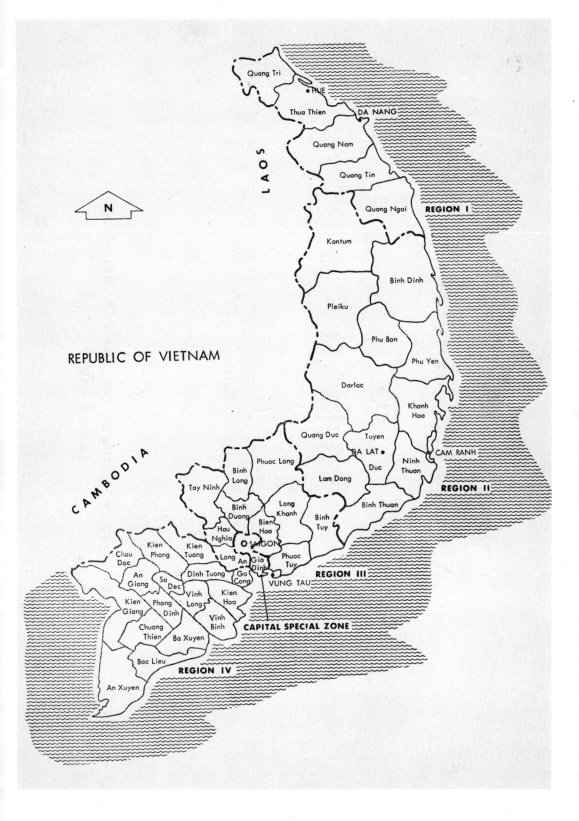

N

REPUBLIC OF VIETNAM

CAMBODIA

LAOS

Quang Tri

• HUE

Thua Thien

DA NANG

Quang Nam

Quang Tin

Quang Ngai

REGION I

Kontum

Binh Dinh

Pleiku

Phu Bon

Phu Yen

Darlac

Khanh Hoa

Quang Duc

Tuyen Duc

DA LAT •

CAM RANH

Phuoc Long

Lam Dong

Ninh Thuan

REGION II

Binh Long

Tay Ninh

Binh Duong

Long Khanh

Binh Thuan

Bien Hoa

Binh Tuy

Hau Nghia

Kien Phong

Kien Tuong

Long An

O SAIGON

Gia Dinh

Phuoc Tuy

Chau Doc

Dinh Tuong

Go Cong

VUNG TAU

REGION III

An Giang

Sa Dec

Vinh Long

Kien Hoa

Kien Giang

Phong Dinh

CAPITAL SPECIAL ZONE

Chuong Thien

Vinh Binh

Ba Xuyen

Bac Lieu

REGION IV

An Xuyen

Chapter I

LAND OF THE DRAGON

As far as the eye can see to the north and the south, no trace of man's existence mars the beautiful golden sand beaches sprinkled with seashells and bits of coral from the blue waters of the South China Sea. Behind you, a short distance inland, the ancient mountains rise from the dense forest. Worn round by centuries of monsoon rains, they lie covered in a thick mat of vegetation, except for the occasional area of rock outcropping too stubborn to hide its face from the sun.

Can this place of peace and tranquility be Hawaii, or perhaps some other Polynesian paradise?

No, this is the "Land of the Dragon," the much-talked-about, supposedly war-ravaged, battle-scarred country of Vietnam.

You are not in the land of the news reporter now. You are far from the densely populated cities on a lonely stretch of Vietnam's 1,650 miles of some of the most beautiful seacoast in the world.

Beautiful unspoiled beaches are everywhere along the 1,650 miles of the South China Sea that forms the eastern boundary of Vietnam.

A few large cities such as Haiphong, Da Nang and Nha Tang and many small cities, villages and hamlets are located on this long coastline. In between the centers of population are hundreds of miles of uninhabited, picturesque coast.

In many areas along the coast the centuries of monsoon rains have cut broad valleys in the mountains and created fertile deltas along the coast. Here the farmer plants his crops in some of the richest rice-growing land in the world. Nearly 80 percent of

12

A fisherman pulls in his long net to harvest gifts of the sea.

the people of Vietnam are farmers, most of them rice farmers.

The numerous streams and rivers wash food into the ocean, encouraging a bountiful supply of fish. Over 190,000 fishermen are engaged in harvesting this crop of the sea in South Vietnam. The fishing industry adds numerous small villages along the coast to those primarily concerned with agriculture.

Unfortunately, the many years of war have made vast expanses of coast and other areas unsafe for habitation. Many small villages have been abandoned and large areas of good land lie unproductive.

The war seems nonexistent here on our lonely stretch of beach, but its effects are ever-present. The barren trees in neat rows were once tenderly cared for by loving hands that encouraged them to produce

Fertile valleys and river deltas along the coast provide rich soil and plentiful water for growing rice, Vietnam's chief product.

succulent fruit. The tumbled remains of old buildings once housed a factory for bottling over a million bottles a year of mineral water from the nearby Vinh Hoa springs. The long row of stones extending out into the water had served as a barrier to protect the many boats that had fished these waters.

In spite of the loss of large areas of the country due to insecurity, South Vietnam today produces more rice and harvests more fish than ever before in its history. Newer varieties of rice, imported from the Philippines, motors for boats, nylon nets and a

Water for rice, water for transportation, water for fishing, water everywhere. This is the Mekong River delta, richest rice-producing area in Vietnam.

hard-working people eager for new knowledge have increased overall productivity in spite of adverse conditions.

A short trip to the south produced a complete change in our surroundings. The land around us is as flat as a table in all directions. Water seems to be everywhere. The water-filled rice fields, ditches and streams leave only narrow trails and roads for travel. Small bushes and clumps of trees surround numerous low islands in this world of water. Here the farmer has his family and livestock housed in buildings constructed mostly of wooden poles covered with rice straw.

15

This is the delta of the Mekong River and the rice bowl of Vietnam, richest rice-producing area in all of Southeast Asia.

Here life is good and food is plentiful. Small orchards and coconut groves add to the rice supply. Chickens, ducks and pigs supply meat for the table and market. Fish are plentiful in the streams and ponds. The children of the dragon live much as they have lived for thousands of years. Water buffalo and oxen still pull the plows and carts. Water is drawn by hand from wells and the small charcoal pots prepare the meals. An occasional three-wheeled Lambreta, a noisy Honda or a blaring transistor radio remind us that we are still in the twentieth century.

A brief journey to the west and to the north again completely changes our surroundings. The morning air is chilly as the sun tries vainly to pierce the triple canopy of vegetation. Lush, green growth surrounds us and seems to add a green hue to the clear mountain air. Overhead the trees entwine and form a thick mat that blocks out the sky.

As the day progresses, the air becomes hot and laden with moisture that makes our clothes cling to the skin and breathing noticeably more difficult.

In the clearing ahead, barking dogs and dark-skinned, naked children greet us. The "long houses" on their high platforms, the definite difference in clothing, language, skin coloration and body structure clearly indicates that we are in a totally differ-

Oxen are still the most common source of power for the farmer.

ent culture. Time has again turned back the pages of history; back to an existence of hunting, fishing and slash-and-burn agriculture. These are the hill tribes that populate the central highlands, scraping out a meager existence from the high plateaus and steaming jungles. They are as unlike the lowland Vietnamese as the Australian Aborigine is unlike other Australians.

In recent years, missionaries, the French, the Americans and the Vietnamese government have brought change into their lives. Caught between the

17

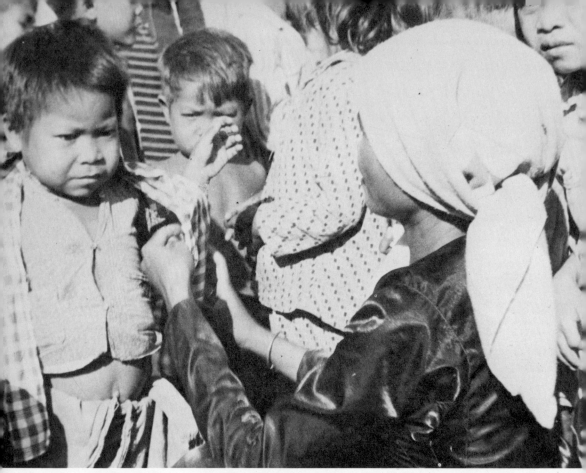

Warm clothing from the missionaries is a welcome protection against the chilly night air in the highlands.

Viet Cong and the government forces of South Vietnam, they have been forced to move near the centers of population. Here they are unable to live in the old way of hunting and mixed agriculture. Though some have been absorbed into the general Vietnamese culture, racial prejudice and a resistance to change has resulted in large numbers of them living in refugee status. Their children are being educated and the old traditions are fading. Unless peace comes soon, they will probably never completely return to their old ways of life.

Prior to the division of the country in 1954, North Vietnam was the center of higher education and manufacturing. South Vietnam was largely agricultural.

The division of the country resulted in the necessity of establishing a system of higher education and industrialization in South Vietnam and a greater reliance on the agricultural development of the Red River Valley delta in the North.

Vietnam shares a common border with China in the north and with Laos and Cambodia in the west. The 1,650 miles of coast extend in an S curve from the north to the south. Near the center of the curve, the country is little more than 25 miles wide, but at either end it widens irregularly to a maximum of 300 miles in the north and 130 miles in the south. Its total land area of 127,000 square miles is about equal to the size of the state of New Mexico in the United States.

In 1954, the country was divided provisionally into approximately two equal parts by the Geneva Conference. The demarcation line follows the Song Ben Hai River from its mouth on the eastern coast to the village of Bo Ho Su, then due west to the Laotian border. The nearness of the 17th parallel to the demarcation line has resulted in reference to the 17th parallel as being the dividing line.

The Red River delta of the north and the Mekong delta of the south contain the major portion of Viet-

19

River taxies propelled by a single shully oar wait for passengers or freight.

Bicycles, Lambrettas, small French taxies and pony carts keep traffic moving at a leisurely pace.

A treat for the Montagnard children assures an eager welcome on the next visit of the traveling medical team.

nam's population. The narrow strip of land connecting these two major areas is composed of mountainous plateaus on the west and a fertile strip of land along the coast.

Approximately sixteen million people live to the north of the 17th parallel and fourteen million to the south. Three fourths of the country's area is sparsely settled uplands and mountainous regions with large areas virtually uninhabited.

Although 80 percent of the people reside in rural areas, about 90 percent of them live on the 13 percent of the land which is best suited for rice production. The result is overcrowding in some areas and also vast expanses of uninhabited wilderness.

Two great rivers serve Vietnam. The 2,800-mile-long Mekong River extends from the mountains of Tibet through China, Burma, Laos, Thailand, Cambodia and Vietnam, then empties into the sea, forming the fertile Mekong Delta.

The Red River of North Vietnam flows for 730 miles from China to its mouth in the Red River Delta.

Travel in Vietnam is difficult due to the present hostilities. The trans-Vietnam railroad which runs from Saigon in the south through Hanoi in the north and connects to the rail system of China is no longer in operation. Few oceangoing vessels carry passengers, and travel by bus, though available, is dangerous. Explosives in the road, ambushes and Viet Cong tax collection points restrict road travel

Tin roofs and toys with wheels in a hill tribe village are significant of the change that is gradually taking place in this centuries-old form of culture.

Thousands of small motorized sailing boats carry cargo along the coast.

to local residents and the more adventurous souls. Air Vietnam has an extensive flight service to all major cities in South Vietnam, but requires considerable advanced booking.

The country offers a good potential as a tourist attraction in the future when hostilities cease.

The Land of the Dragon and its attractive, polite, industrious people offer a touch of the Orient that has a unique quality unlike that found elsewhere.

Chapter II

TWO THOUSAND YEARS OF CULTURAL DEVELOPMENT

Perhaps four thousand years ago . . . for who can be sure about legends . . . a descendant of one of the great emperors of China took a journey to the south into the land now known as Vietnam. There he met a Tien or spirit of great beauty, and a son was born of their union. This son reigned over the land and married the daughter of the God of the Sea. Their son, who was named Lac Long or Fox Dragon, fought off the Chinese invaders and later took to wife the mountain spirit Au Co. She bore him one hundred sons. Lac Long took fifty sons to live with him by the sea and Au Co took fifty sons to live with her in the mountains. These were the ancestors of the Vietnamese of today, or so the story goes.

This tale is taught to children in school and is accepted more as fact than as legend.

25

Peace memorial erected in Phan Thiet.

Statues in the courtyard of the citadel at Hue, the old capital.

Scholars seeking a more factual basis to explain the origin of their people have turned to archaeology as a possible source of information. Large bronze drums similar to those found in the Philippines, Thailand, Indonesia and the Pacific islands seem to indicate that the Vietnamese ancestors may have been of Melanesian and Indonesian background.

Historical Chinese documents dating back to 500 B.C. describe Vietnam as the southernmost province of China and proclaim the people to be a mixture of Chinese and the Malayo-Indonesian people then lo-

The memory of Phu Dong Thien Vung is preserved in this statue erected in his honor in Saigon.

cated farther to the south. At this point in time, Vietnam did not extend as far south as the Red River delta. Considerable fighting took place as the southern movement was extended to include much of what is today known as North Vietnam. The Chinese succeeded in conquering the Vietnamese people and ruled Vietnam for one thousand years. During this period several revolutions occurred which restored independence for brief periods of time. This was a time of great heroes.

The most notable of the rebellions was led by two of the most remarkable women in Vietnamese history, the Trung sisters, Trung Trau and Trung Nhi. They formed a huge army and succeeded in driving out the Chinese in A.D. 39. They then ruled jointly as queens of the land until A.D. 43 when they drowned themselves upon learning that their armies were again defeated by the Chinese. Their memory is a cherished one today with many streets and public places named in their honor. Hai Ba Trung, the name of an important street in Saigon, means Two Trung Women.

In A.D. 248, another Vietnamese woman rose clad in golden armor, to lead the rebel armies, riding on an elephant before an army of a thousand men. This revolt was not successful and Thieu Au, perhaps remembering the Trung sisters, took her own life.

Revolution followed revolution until the Chinese were finally defeated by General Ngo Quyen. Several Vietnamese rulers followed, each extending his rule farther south into the Champa kingdom. Years of fierce fighting resulted in the conquering of the Chams and the extension of Vietnam as far south as present-day Saigon.

The Vietnamese are quick to adapt to new ideas and learned much from those who dominated them. Chinese agricultural methods, mathematics, schools and the Mandarin system of government were retained as a part of their culture.

Seven dragons stand guard over the Buddha of the fisherman at Phan Thiet.

In 1284, Kublai Khan, the terrible Chinese war-lord, attacked Vietnam with 500,000 men. Tran Hung Dao, leading 200,000 men, successfully repelled the attack on the banks of the Bach Dang River in the same place and using the same tactics that were used by Ngo Quyen three hundred and fifty years earlier to defeat the Chinese.

Although Tran won a brilliant victory, the after-effects were to prove fatal. The war had seriously weakened the country and in a few years the Chinese, under the cruel Ming Dynasty, again ruled the land. Twenty years of bitter oppression followed. The Vietnamese writer Nguyen Trai wrote, "Indeed, all the water of the Eastern Sea hardly seemed

30

Chinese influence is evident in the design of this water tower at Phan Thiet.

enough to wash away the stains; all the bamboos of the southern mountains insufficient to record the crimes committed."

The people rose behind the leadership of LeLoi, and, using guerrilla tactics, drove out the Chinese for the last time.

The Vietnamese leaders who followed extended the boundaries of Vietnam to the present limits at the tip of the Mekong Delta by defeating the Cambodians who lived there and claimed the land for themselves. During this period, two opposing Vietnamese dynasties, the Nguyen and the Trinh, divided the country into a north and a south Vietnam by building a huge stone wall a few miles from the same boundary that divides the country today.

The Portuguese began to sell arms to the Nguyen and the Dutch sold arms to the Trinh. In 1673, a truce was declared and the country was again united, but Western foreign intervention had begun.

French missionaries arrived in Vietnam and began to strongly influence the people.

The Vietnamese emperor Minh Long feared the influence of the missionaries and began to persecute them. This aroused the indignation of the French people and resulted in war with the French. In 1882, a treaty was signed making all of Vietnam a French possession. The French soon ruled all of Indochina, which also included Cambodia and Laos.

While in power, the French built roads, improved the cities, built a national railroad, established uni-

A Chinese temple in Saigon erected for worship by the large number of Chinese who reside there.

Hundreds of Vietnamese received a new lease on life from the skilled hands of these doctors from Taiwan who volunteered their services to provide much-needed medical aid to Vietnamese civilians.

versities and other schools and greatly developed the country. This development benefited the French, but did little for the Vietnamese people except for a handful of wealthy Vietnamese who served the French.

During World War II, the Japanese easily conquered Vietnam and co-existed with the French until the war was nearly over.

After the war, the French again dominated Vietnam. The Viet Minh, who for years had fought the French in unsuccessful guerrilla warfare, now had arms and trained men from World War II. They defeated the French in 1954 at Dienbien Phu.

The Geneva Conference which followed provisionally divided the country at the demarcation zone and created the present Democratic Republic of Vietnam or North Vietnam and the Republic of Vietnam or South Vietnam.

Peace lasted only for a short time and war between North and South Vietnam began.

Russia and China supplied arms and technical assistance to North Vietnam. The United States, Korea, Australia, Thailand and the Philippines supplied men, arms and technical assistance to South Vietnam.

After eighteen years of fighting and the loss of hundreds of thousands of lives, the war still continues.

The people of Vietnam are a tremendously nationalistic people. They are proud of their Vietnamese heritage and their "two thousand years of culture." Regardless of whether a Vietnamese favors the government of North or South Vietnam, he is first a Vietnamese, proud of his heroes, steeped in legend and tradition and very much in love with his land.

Orphans are usually cared for by relatives. The few children that are in orphanages appear to be happy and receiving excellent care.

Chapter III

FOLKLORE AND TRADITION

"The Vietnamese live on rice and legends and myths," is an ancient saying from this fascinating and beautiful land of Vietnam.

Folklore reveals a people's basic beliefs and yearnings, sheds light on their search for greater truths and exposes those values they wish to bequeath to their children. A nation's folktales thus have a significance beyond their storytelling beauty.

Folklore in Vietnam serves much the same purpose as fairy tales did in the past in the United States. What better way is there to hold the attention of the youth and at the same time instill in them basic "truths" or nationalistic premises?

A study of Vietnamese folklore reveals many tales similar to those of other nations. The actions of the characters are changed to coincide with Oriental concepts.

For example, consider the following: A man lost his wife and remarried. His daughter was not liked

A Vietnamese family with baskets of gifts are on their way to greet friends on "Tet," the Vietnamese New Year.

by his new wife who showed greater favor to the new daughter she presented him. Tam, the first daughter, was forced to work in the kitchen most of the time and to do the heavy work.

The midautumn festival arrived and the stepmother ordered Tam to stay home. A goddess appeared, and, taking various common objects, converted them into beautiful clothing. At the festival, she caught the eye of the king, and when people began admiring her and whispering about her she became frightened and ran away. In the process she lost one of her slippers. The king found it and ordered

Movies and theatrical performances are usually related to folktales or earlier periods of Vietnamese history, and are accompanied by hero, heroine, villain, and a good deal of sword fighting.

his men to find the girl it fit, which they did. Tam and the king were married and lived happily ever after. The mother and stepsister were so angry that they burst their blood vessels and died. This tale is very nearly a duplicate of Cinderella, which we all know.

Other folktales seem to exist as a reminder to children to behave well. Such a tale is "The Spirit of the Hearth."

In every home, the spirits of the characters of the tale are assigned to watch over the hearth (cooking area). It is considered rude to make noises in their presence. Children are taught to be quiet in the area of the hearth. Since the typical country home has only one or two rooms, this could be inferred as meaning that children should be quiet inside the home.

In my two years in Vietnam, only on two occasions did I hear a child cry or speak loudly in a home or even near it. At play in the street or on the school playground they are as noisy as any other children.

The array of folktales is numerous, serving many purposes: teaching proper behavior, reminding the wife of her husband's superior position in the family, reminding the husband of his duty to his family and ancestors, explaining natural phenomena, and others.

Folklore served the same purpose to the American Indian and to peoples throughout the world in less-developed areas where formal schooling is often not available.

In Vietnam the folktale remains a sort of "fairy tale" to the educated, and a real part of life to the less educated. The Westerner often makes the mistake of believing the more educated, when he says he doesn't really believe in folktales. He probably, deep down inside, believes.

Educated Westerners know it is ridiculous to believe in bad luck as a result of walking under a ladder, but usually avoid it when possible. Breaking a

Drawings on a temple wall relate tales of past centuries.

Painted eyes guide Vietnamese navy boats.

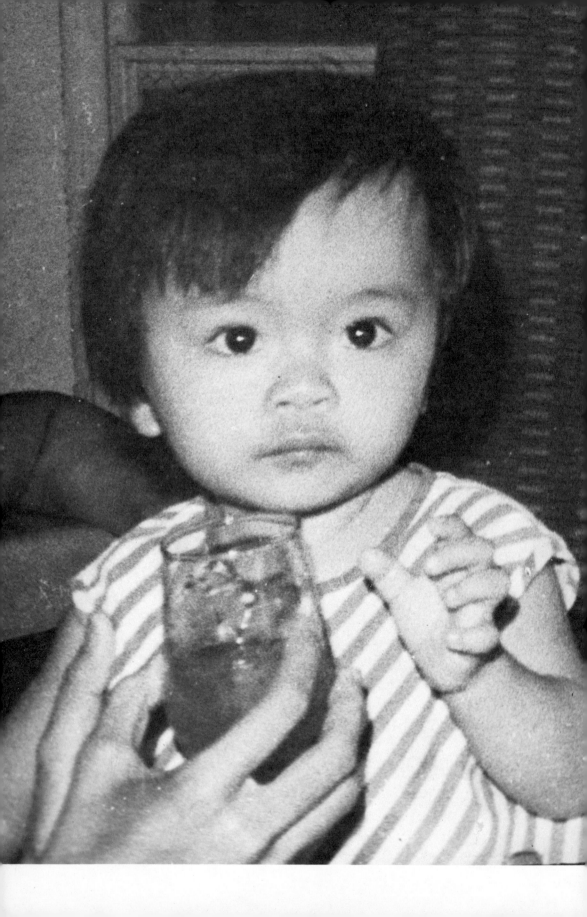

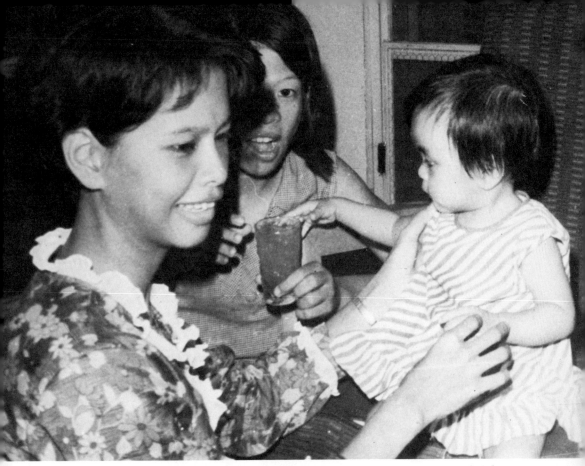
Vietnamese children seldom cry. Their every need is continually satisfied by constant care by adults or older siblings.

mirror or having a black cat cross your path isn't really bad luck, but somehow it does tend to make one feel a little uneasy. As sophisticated as we may think we are, we, too, have our beliefs in folklore and superstitions, but we seldom care to admit it.

Much of the folklore of Vietnam is of Chinese origin. The thousand years of Chinese domination, the use of the Chinese language by Vietnamese scholars for two thousand years, the forced use of Chinese writing due to the former lack of a written form for Vietnamese, and the Mandarin system of education all contributed to this influx of Chinese tales into Vietnamese folklore.

The Vietnamese people have great respect for beauty and love music and poetry.

Poetry is a part of their daily lives at whatever level of education they may be. They like to make up poems when friends gather together, and consider it a pleasant way to spend an evening. Even the illiterate often memorize verses of the national poem, Kim Van Kiew. They turn to poetry for quotations when in a romantic mood, for comfort in difficult situations, and for good and bad omens to foretell the future.

Poets, artists, actors and other talented individuals are highly respected, sometimes to the point of being exempt from military duty and from paying taxes.

It is not uncommon for a Vietnamese man to retire from work at the age of forty or even younger and spend his time writing poetry while his family works to support him and themselves. In our society he would be considered lazy. In Vietnam it is considered quite normal. A man who can read the stars and predict the future is also highly respected. Important meetings and trips are sometimes canceled because the stars or some other sign has predicted that it is a bad day for such a venture.

In Vietnam, as in our country, certain acts are considered bad luck or bad manners. Pointing your

The guitar and Western music are giving serious competition to the old traditional music, much to the concern of the elders.

toe at someone or at the family altar when you are seated is considered very bad manners. The head is considered as the home of the soul by Buddhists; therefore, it is not proper to place your hand on someone's head.

The Vietnamese realize that visitors to their country do not understand their customs and are not offended when the visitor does not follow them. Taking the time to learn proper behavior according to their customs will, in Vietnam as elsewhere, make you much more welcome.

In the larger cities the old ways are being forgotten to some extent and Westernization has become more accepted.

In Saigon, it is a common sight to see a boy and a girl riding together on a bicycle or motor bike. In the country, boys and girls do not date before they are married. Marriages are often arranged by the parents and a girl may be promised to a boy long before they are old enough to marry. If a boy is allowed to visit a girl before they are married, they are closely chaperoned. If a boy wishes to marry a girl, he will not ask her, he will have his parents ask her parents. If the parents agree, the boy will come to visit the girl, bringing a gift for the girl's family. Often, he will also bring the traditional betel nut, as has been the custom for years. In Vietnam it is against the law for an unmarried girl to walk on the street or ride in a vehicle with a man from another country.

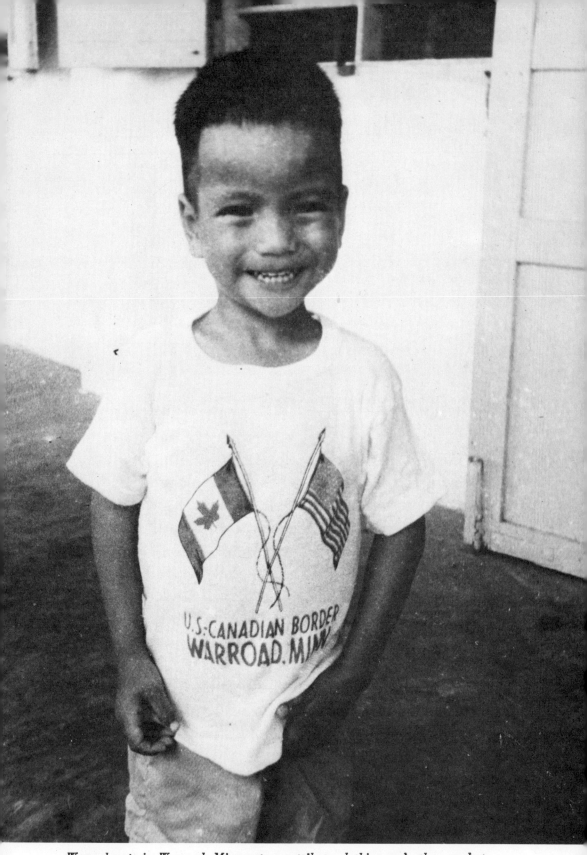

Warm hearts in Warroad, Minnesota, contribute clothing and other goods to Vietnam orphans.

Ceremonies and inspections are an important part of life and accompany the dedication of all public buildings, wells, roads and other projects as well as all holidays and special occasions.

Family ties are very close in Vietnam. The family more than the individual is the basic unit of Vietnam's society. It embraces the dead as well as the living, tying past generations to those still alive and to those yet to come. Each member, in death as in life, assumes his place in this scheme of things, according to his rank. The family includes all those who are directly descended through the male line from the same ancestors.

Obedience to parents is almost complete. The writer has known Vietnamese friends who married when and who their parents said to marry. Others gave up dearly sought scholarships in the United States because their parents said they would be

Mother seldom needs to be concerned about the younger children. This is the duty of the next oldest child or grandmother if she lives in the same house.

lonely without them. Some turn down high-paying jobs in other cities because their parents do not want them to leave. Marriage or age change nothing in an individual's devotion and obedience to his parents.

Children of the same family show great devotion to each other. Everywhere one sees young children carrying around younger children, sometimes almost as large as they are. The mother, or more often the grandmother, provides care for the older children who in turn take care of the younger children when they become old enough. Everywhere they go the younger ones tag along or are carried. Rarely do you see them argue with or mistreat their brothers and sisters. It is not uncommon for one or more members of a family to contribute a large part of their earnings for long periods of time so a brother or sister can get an education, even though they themselves are not educated. This devotion to family seems to be a genuine product of family love without resentment or self-pity.

There is little need for massive welfare programs in Vietnam, except for those who have been uprooted from their homes by the war. Families stick together and look after each other, providing for parents or brother or sister as the need arises.

It is indeed unfortunate that this meritorious benevolence seems to lose importance as a country's standard of living increases.

Chapter IV

THE VILLAGE—HEART OF GOVERNMENTAL STRUCTURE

There is an old saying in Vietnam that "The Emperor's rule stops at the village gate." The village was the traditional focal point of the Vietnamese culture in the past. A village is composed of two or more hamlets, each with its own hamlet officials. The officials of the hamlet have little authority other than that given to them by the village council. The size of villages varies considerably in both land area and in population.

A council of notables in each village presided over all matters pertaining to the welfare of the villagers and was responsible to the government for the collection of taxes and conformity to the laws of the country. They decided how the tax burden was to be divided among the people, who would farm the plots of common land, which lands would be set aside to feed the poor, to help the old, the sick, the wid-

Phu Long, a typical country village, surrounded by fields of rice.

owed, to care for families while their men were in the army and to support students while they studied.

Each village had its central meeting hall and its temple for the worship of the village spirit. In short, the village provided for all the vital needs of the people of that village.

Each village also had an assortment of public, private and secret groups formed for various purposes. Most villages had a secret militant group that in time of strife or oppression could join groups from other villages to combat the common threat. Thus, the village-based guerrilla movement of our times is an extension of a very old tradition.

Village and hamlet officials attend a training session to prepare them in performing their duties.

The Mong Mon River winds lazily through the city of Phan Thìet on its way to the sea. The city is composed of several independent villages which combine to give it a population of over 90,000.

Not all functions of the village were beneficial, however. It was difficult for strangers to enter into the village social structure. The village, while preserving the Vietnamese heritage, also barred the way to progress at every level, whether intellectual or technical.

The people of the village grew so dependent upon the village to run their lives and take care of their needs that they became overly dependent and did little decisionmaking for themselves. When circumstances required leaving the village or the village structure was destroyed, the villagers were practically lost and their society crumbled. The Chinese respected the sanction of the village and did little to destroy its function.

The French disrupted the organization by establishing districts with district chiefs in each province. Hereafter, the district, not the village, was the focal point of government. Village councils had little or no authority and served only as figureheads with no real power.

In a society where most of the people identify with their village, even though they may have left it years ago, this movement of the French did much to create antagonism toward them.

When the people organized to rebel against the French, they did so by forming an organization called the Viet Minh. The Viet Minh secretly elected their own village officials and reestablished their own

Cattle forage for their own food and produce a supply of stringy beef for the local market.

Some villages are composed of a few mud and thatched huts along the road while others have modern buildings and populations numbering in the thousands.

government on the village level in keeping with the old traditions.

After the defeat of the French, some of the Viet Minh joined allegiance with the Republic of Vietnam (South Vietnam) and many of them are today holding major political and military positions. Others chose to oppose the new government and reorganized, calling themselves the National Liberation Front, more popularly known as the Viet Cong. Their organization depended on the Democratic Republic of Vietnam (North Vietnam) for arms and more manpower. North Vietnam's leader, Ho Chi Minh, turned to Red China and Russia for assistance.

When the United States became involved in Vietnam, the U. S., through President Diem, placed emphasis on the hamlet level with the "strategic hamlet" program. Again the village became almost a nonentity with the hamlet and the old French district system receiving all the attention and power.

In 1969, after years of frustration and lack of real progress, the Vietnamese government, with United States encouragement, reorganized their approach and made the village again the focal point of local government. One million piasters (U. S. $8,466) was allocated to each village with elected officials. (Most villages elected officials in 1968 and 1969. Binh Thuan province, with which the writer is familiar, had elected officials in 50 of the 53 villages.)

In the 1969 program, the village council formed a committee of representatives of the various groups

56

Small herds of sheep and goats add protein to the diet of Cham villages.

within the village such as the elders, the farmers, the teachers, etc. This group of representatives decided what the village needed, how much money to allocate to each project, how much money they would try to raise by local contributions, how much labor had to be hired and how much labor they thought they could count on the people to donate. With this plan drawn, complete with project deadlines, they summoned all the people of the village, explained the plan and asked for their approval or suggestions for modification. When the final ap-

57

This new well, the result of a village "self-help project," provides much-needed water for bathing and drinking.

A ceremony is held to officially recognize the completion of a new village road.

proval of the villagers was received, the plan was sent to the provincial government and funds were allocated on a project basis. If a large project costing over a million piasters is needed, additional funds may be requested, subject to the province chief's and Saigon's approval.

This program has met with great enthusiasm at the village level and shows signs of successful implementation. For the first time since before the French, the people again feel that they have a voice in their own affairs.

This new program has some problems which will have to be settled if the program is to be successful.

Prior to the 1969 village development program, each provincial education chief decided how many elementary classrooms were needed for the next year and how many teachers were needed. The Ministry of Education in Saigon would approve the plan or modify it as they felt necessary, and issued the funds needed for implementation.

Under the present plan, the village decides if it wants to build classrooms or not. The education chief has no voice in the matter. The education chief in Binh Thuan province sent letters to all village chiefs recommending the number of classrooms and the number of teachers that would be needed. Most villages followed his recommendations, but some refused to do so. At a village meeting this writer attended in Go Boi hamlet, the village council insisted

Fishing along the coast is best at night. During the day, fishermen spread their nets on racks or over the masts to dry.

Fresh water is often a problem, especially in the dry central coast areas. The round woven reed container in the boat holds fresh drinking water from far upstream.

Young and old alike gather to hear the plans of the Village Development Committee that they have chosen to represent them in deciding what is most needed to improve their village.

Sanitation workers spread insecticides to help control flies.

on building two more classrooms and wanted two more teachers. The education chief explained that they had only twenty-five students per classroom, and a teacher for each class. They didn't need additional personnel or facilities. In spite of his recommendation, they decided to continue with their plans.

Education is highly regarded in Vietnam, and having more classrooms than necessary is looked upon as being highly prestigious even though the funds can be better used elsewhere. It is also possible that a village council may decide not to build classrooms even though they are needed. In the end, common sense will probably take over, as it usually does.

As this writer traveled throughout Binh Thuan province, scores of requests for funds for countless projects, some ridiculous, but most essential, were brought to his attention. Villagers seemed to feel that only Americans had solutions to their problems and the necessary funds. After repeated argument and long discussion, they usually came around to believing that funds and materials were available only upon request through their own governmental channels and proceeded to find their own solutions to pressing problems. Solutions often resulted in two hundred to three hundred people volunteering their labor and contributing their funds to get the job done. They mainly needed technical assistance and the assurance that their funds would be used for the intended purposes. They trusted Americans and felt

USAID headquarters for Binh Thuan Province served as a coordinating, reporting and advising center for U. S. civilian and military advisors on the 179-man "Advisory Team No. 37."

"An old Asian hand," Chester A. Richardson has served as an advisor in Vietnam for eight years. He is known and admired throughout Vietnam as a capable leader and a good friend by both Vietnamese and Americans. He is ably assisted by his companions, Oliver Modronal and Ceasar Torres, from the Philippines.

that the job would get done if an American advisor were involved.

At times a vital project had eager volunteers available, but due to the poverty of the particular area, no funds. Somehow, through scrounging, raiding military dumps, begging, borrowing and occasionally confiscating, the materials showed up and projects were completed. The 1969 village development plan provided much-needed funds and a means of accomplishment for many plans not otherwise possible. With a little assistance, new roads, bridges, rice and net-drying racks, classrooms, wells and other necessities became available through the cooperative effort of the people. Life goes on now, a little better than before, and once again the village structure prevails.

Here are one's ancestors, one's roots and security. Here is where a man longs to be and dreams of returning if he is forced to leave. Governments change and time passes by, but the village now, as in centuries past, remains the heart of Vietnam.

Chapter V

A LAND DIVIDED

Obstacles to progress must be overcome before Vietnam can achieve the goal of national unity under a representative government offering equal opportunity for all of its people.

The division of the country by the Geneva Conference has resulted in a split in political ideology and serious wounds that will be long in healing if the country is reunited. Socialism, Communism, Capitalism and Democracy represent political ideals that cannot comfortably survive together. Whether one ideology or a combination will survive, only time can tell.

Aside from the differences in political convictions, numerous other barriers to real unity are present. The Vietnamese language is spoken by at least 85 percent of the population. Dialects within the language often present problems in communication and at times make real communication impossible even though both parties speak Vietnamese.

Monsoon rains flood streets and cause problems in the city, but bring much-needed moisture to the rice paddies in the country.

Boats, trucks, buses and air transportation are limited, and oxen, pony carts and manpower must be utilized to move most products to centralized markets.

Three major variations of the language exist: Northern, Central, and Southern Vietnamese, with countless local variations and colloquialisms. The writer has been in situations where a Vietnamese interpreter had to be used to translate one dialect of Vietnamese into another as well as Vietnamese into English in order to clearly conduct the business at hand. Even then it was not clear whether or not all persons involved understood.

The non-Vietnamese minorities, of which the Chinese are the most numerous, use their own languages among themselves. The one million or so Chinese speak a variety of Chinese dialects. Most Chinese also speak Vietnamese, especially since a law was passed requiring the teaching of the Vietnamese language in all minority schools.

The balance of the ethnic groups is composed primarily of Montagnards, Chams, Indians, Pakistanis, French and Americans. Many do not speak Vietnamese.

No accurate census has ever been taken of the Montagnard (hill tribes) population of Vietnam. Estimates for both North and South Vietnam run as high as three million.

Years of isolation from the balance of the population has resulted in little knowledge of the Vietnamese language. As many as thirty-five different dialects are spoken by the Montagnards, most of them so different from one another that no communi-

Temporary camps could not hold the 44,000 new refugees that sought shelter in Phan Thiet during the 1968 Tet offensive. Tent cities sprang up in vacant lots to house the surplus.

Shacks made of tin and scrap sprang up overnight in city streets when incoming refugees arrived faster than government workers could handle them.

Bicycle wheels and parts add pedal power to manpower on this delivery cart.

cation is possible. No written forms exist for the many dialects. An attempt to produce a written form of some of the major dialects is presently being made by missionaries.

In Vietnam, as in most other countries, racial prejudice is also an influencing factor. Until recent years, the Montagnards were not included in the government, education or welfare systems. This was partially a result of racial prejudice and partially due to a lack of interest in becoming involved in lowland affairs on the part of the Montagnards.

The Catholic Cathedral of Notre Dame in Saigon raises twin Gothic spires to the sky. Kennedy Square, in front, was named in memory of United States President John F. Kennedy.

The Chinese tend to dominate the economic community and prefer to associate with Chinese. The Chinese and Vietnamese seldom intermarry or associate socially. The Vietnamese prefer to stay apart from the Chinese except for business purposes. Normally the Chinese live together in their own area of a village, and because of their involvement in the business world they are found in most cities of any size. The Montagnards, Nungs and Chams also usually live apart from the Vietnamese in their own villages.

Approximately 80 percent of the Vietnamese are Buddhist. To say that one is Buddhist in Vietnam is a generalization, not a specific declaration. Among the Buddhists, 90 percent claim to be Mahayan and 10 percent claim to be Thenóvada. However, even within these groups many variations exist. Though they claim to be Buddhist, Confucianism and Taoism have had their influence as well, creating a form of Buddhism that is unique to Vietnam and varies from place to place within the country.

Confucianism, Taoism, Catholicism, the Cao Dai, the Hoa Hao, along with various forms of Animism and other religions comprise the religious aspirations of much of the balance of the population.

Religion in itself can be viewed as a positive factor in the lives of people, but when it separates them into groups who isolate themselves from each other, the effect can be detrimental to national progress.

Imported apples that cannot be raised in Vietnam's tropical climate compete with local fruit in the market.

Montagnard tribesmen in lowland refugee settlements attend schools, wear modern clothing, and learn new ways to make a living. They will probably never return to their more primitive way of life in the highlands.

U. S. Army helicopters provide transportation for Vietnamese who prefer to move to refugee camps in secure areas instead of living in the danger of the countryside.

The atheistic aspect of communist philosophy has in recent years resulted in a closer association of the various religious factions. Most religious leaders look upon the Viet Cong as a threat to organized religion.

The attitude of indifference toward rural affairs displayed by urban dwellers, particularly when one considers that most government officials are from the cities, also presents serious problems. Only in recent years have government officials realized that they must cease to consider the rural villagers as socially inferior and a source of manpower for agricultural exploitation and military conscription. This attitude was partially responsible for the support given to the Viet Cong by those in rural areas. The 1969 village development program has done much to overcome this handicap.

The basic traditions and customs of the Vietnamese people in their relationships to each other and to foreigners also present certain problems which make communications and interpersonal relationships difficult.

One reason many Westerners are frustrated and ineffective in their relationships in Vietnam is that they fail to look beyond the veneer of Westernization in language and education to the more fundamental aspects of the national character. Our way of looking at a situation may have no meaning to a Vietnamese. At times their reasons for acting as they do do not make sense to us.

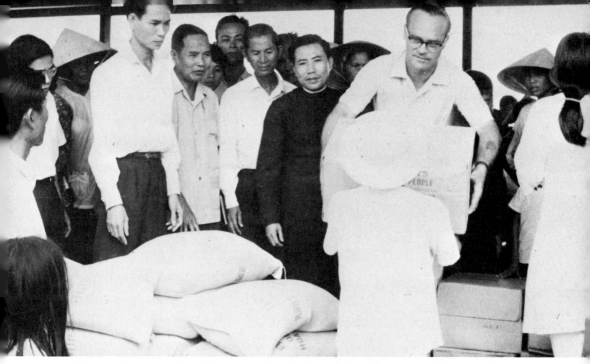

New refugees receive U. S. surplus food and building materials to make homes. Most refugees are self-sufficient in a few months. Many will return to their former homes when security is better.

Army trucks haul water to refugees.

When working with the Vietnamese one must always keep in mind that they are an extremely polite people with definite rules and restrictions on their relationships with others. These restrictions may prevent them from saying exactly what they wish to say and, therefore, they may appear to be in agreement when they are not. They may not answer truthfully for fear that the truth is not what you want to hear, and they want to please you. Deadlines and time schedules are looked upon as suggestions rather than as something to be closely followed. Tomorrow often turns out to be next week or next month or a polite way of saying "I don't want to do what you ask."

When you are offering an explanation, you cannot assume that the other person understands. He may say he does when he has no idea what you are talking about because he does not want to admit that his English is not as good as you think it is nor does he want to offend you by letting you know that you are not doing a good job of explaining.

Education is an important goal to most Vietnamese. They know that education is a necessity to advancement in life. Their high regard for education is a good aspect of their culture, but has its detrimental aspects as well.

A Vietnamese will work extremely hard to get an education and considers an educated man to be superior to one without an education. Once he is edu-

A lone Lambretta serves as the only motorized means of transportation for the ten thousand residents of Phu Qui Island that lies ninety miles off shore in the South China Sea.

cated, he feels that he is above manual labor and is not expected to work with his hands.

While working in Vietnam, the writer employed an interpreter who had a college degree. He was an ideal interpreter and a good friend. On three occasions it was necessary for the writer to leave the country. On all three occasions the interpreter refused to work for anyone else until the writer returned. The other Americans were not educated as well as he was, therefore it was beneath his dignity to work for them. He worked without complaint for

Song Mao, in Binh Thuan Province, is the home of the few surviving royalty of the Champa Empire. The man in his turban and gown and the women in their full-length dresses proudly dress as Chams have dressed for centuries.

the writer because the writer had a better education than he did.

On another occasion, it was necessary to transport eight tons of books to remote schools. Transportation was difficult to arrange. After weeks of effort, air transportation was provided with three days advance notice. Even though the education chief had repeatedly pleaded for transportation for the books, he was able to only have one ton ready on time. He explained that though he had twenty-one people working in his office, he had only one man with a poor enough education to do the manual labor of packing and loading books. This attitude presents a serious problem, particularly when an individual is sent to a technical training school for skill training such as auto mechanics or electrical repair, and when trained, develops the attitude that his education exempts him from manual labor and that his job should consist of telling others what to do.

In spite of the many obstacles to national development, good progress is being made. Obstacles to progress are found in all countries, in Vietnam as elsewhere, patience will find a way to overcome them.

Delicate features and a natural beauty are characteristic of Vietnamese women.

Chapter VI

A TIME FOR PLEASURE

Though never expressed verbally, one could readily believe that a standard prayer in Vietnam would include: "Give me the strength to change what I can and to accept that which I cannot change." Patience is a virtue that few Vietnamese lack.

Despite the fact that war has been and still is an almost constant part of their lives for two thousand years and is an everyday threat, life proceeds in an orderly fashion. The people smile, laugh and find time for pleasure. Simple pleasures to be sure, but a basic, down-to-earth appreciation for life and the joy that it holds are a part of their everyday lives.

Everywhere in the country the Vietnamese find time to cheerfully greet friends, smile at a stranger, and enjoy what there is to enjoy.

Movie theaters are crowded, restaurants are found everywhere, all of them doing well. Children laugh, play and chatter incessantly as children do everywhere.

Warm smiles and friendly faces encourage friendship.

Almost everyone has sorrows and problems, not enough money, friends and loved ones lost in the war, countless problems with few exempt. "Troubles are real and ever-present, but right now life is not so bad that we can waste an opportunity to laugh and be gay." This seems to be the prevailing attitude.

Parent-teacher organizations exist in practically every village. Boy Scout troops, Girl Scouts, 4-H Clubs (4-T in Vietnam), numerous other youth groups, tennis, soccer, track teams and athletic organizations of all kinds are found everywhere.

In September, school children from all of the elementary schools make paper lanterns for the Children's Day celebration. At night thousands of lanterns of many shapes and colors parade through the

A meat vendor sells chunks of fresh meat on a city sidewalk.

A soup vendor carries her charcoal burner, soup pot and other equipment.

streets as the children proceed to the city square for the speeches, dragon dancers and entertainment. Prizes are given to the best dancers and to the classes and schools with the best lanterns.

In the spring of the year another elaborate program complete with prizes is held to honor those students who have done well in their studies.

Each of the forty-four provinces of South Vietnam has an office, staff and Chief of Youth and Sports. It is his duty to arrange athletic events, help and advise youth organizations and arrange for festivals. The Chief of Youth and Sports is a highly respected man.

The children seem to be forever busy with some activity or another. Oriental versions of hopscotch, hide and seek, tag, marbles and other games that children play the world over are also the favorites in Vietnam.

Stop for a walk through a rural hamlet and you are soon surrounded by laughing children who have come to see the big hairy man from another land. As you walk along, some of the more bold ones invariably will pull at the hair on your arms to see if it is real. Vietnamese have very little body hair and few find it necessary to shave.

Walk along a street and you are seldom alone. Seemingly from out of nowhere a little hand reaches up and takes yours as a young child joins you on your walk.

Herding cattle is much more pleasant when they are patient enough to give you a ride.

Concrete sewer pipes provide a bit of shade.

Sometimes the children get overly enthusiastic, especially when they find you can speak Vietnamese. Hold out your arm and two or three immediately hang on and swing themselves off the ground as their buddies shriek with laughter. You tire of the fun long before they do and soon some adult will come to the rescue and shoo away the children for a brief moment.

Many Americans, especially the younger military personnel, make the mistake of giving candy or cigarettes to the children. The older people do not like their children to learn to beg and annoy people. Unfortunately, the habit has spread and in the cities the children have learned to follow Americans, begging for candy, cigarettes and money. Some have become proficient in stealing watches, wallets and anything that is handy. Rural children are quite different and seldom beg. If you wish to give a gift to the children, it is proper to first give it to an older Vietnamese person or to their parents to pass out. This meets with the approval of the adults.

Vietnam is administratively divided into four geographic and political regions. In the fall of the year, a region-wide athletic contest is arranged to compete for regional recognition. Transportation is difficult to secure for such large groups of athletes, so not all teams can attend and sometimes the entire event must be canceled.

In 1967, a huge athletic event was held at Phan Rang with hundreds of athletes present from all of

A hole dug in a patch of ground in a sidewalk planter offers a chance fo a game of skill.

A public water faucet provides a cool bath on a hot day.

Sausages, chicken, ducks and other delicacies hang from racks in the marketplace.

the provinces in the II Corps (Region II). The event lasted for three days and covered every event from swimming to cross country bicycling, to soccer, and most other events normally found at such competitions.

The enthusiasm of the people was unbelievable and crowd control became the biggest problem of the day.

Hundreds of children and young adults wanted to test their speed against those competing in the races and at times crowded the field and track to the

Sidewalk restaurants do a brisk business.

point where the contestants had little room for competing. The boxing matches had to be delayed because spectators actually climbed into the ring to see better and there was no room for the boxers. The Korean karate team had little difficulty putting on their exhibition. Whenever the crowd pressed too close, they joined arms and elbowed them back to their places.

Our Binh Thuan province team of eighty athletes returned home in triumph. They had tied for first place in soccer and won thirty-seven other gold medals and trophies. When they returned to Phan Thiet, crowds of people lined the streets to cheer for their favorite athletes and show their support of the teams.

The Vietnamese people love music and theatrical performances. Dozens of groups of actors and musicians travel throughout the country putting on live performances that play to capacity crowds. The plays are usually historical in nature, with ancient dances, sword fights and great amounts of crying as the hero or heroine fights for justice against the cruel Chinese warlords or unjust villains. The performances last for hours, but no one seems to tire of watching.

Lately, television has become a big attraction and many village squares have a TV set for the people to watch. Every evening two hundred to three hundred people gather around to watch their favorite program.

Binh Thuan Province athletes win top honors with thirty-seven gold medals and several trophys.

Binh Thuan soccer team ties for first place.

There are few toys, and those available are expensive. Children use their ingenuity to make their own toys. A beer can, some rubber bands and a stick make an effective, noisy push toy for the little brothers and sisters. The same materials are used to make toy guns with a stick that bangs away on the can when the rubber band unwinds. Tree branches and old tire tubes makes effective slingshots. Bamboo and paper are made into high-flying kites and tightly tied balls of rags make fair soccer balls.

Dancing and drinking alcoholic beverages is not a part of the Vietnamese way of life. Few can afford such luxuries and fewer yet would take part if they could. In the larger cities some night clubs are available, but are mostly attended by foreigners and the soldiers.

Eating at the many restaurants is the main entertainment for those who can afford it. Prices range considerably from very inexpensive from the lady who cooks on a charcoal burner on the sidewalk to very expensive in the indoor restaurants. A good meal will often cost from 600 to 1200 piasters (about $5 to $10). A working man earns about 200 piasters a day and can seldom afford such luxury. In spite of the high prices, the restaurants are often filled to capacity.

Vietnamese cooking is an art in itself. At home, food is usually simple and an average meal consists of rice with a bit of fish or meat and perhaps some

Fishing boats are often available for rent during the day and provide an inexpensive means of sightseeing, skin diving or fishing.

greens or fruit. In the restaurants the menus are pages long with dozens of choices of superbly seasoned food. In the cities, American dishes are available in the larger restaurants. Vietnamese beef and chicken tend to be tough and stringy. Their ducks, pork and seafood are often superior to that found in the United States. Soups are marvels of the culinary art and are usually served family style in large metal bowls with burning charcoal in a cone in the center to keep them piping hot.

It is the custom for the host to pick out the choice bits of foods for his guests. Often a chicken or duck

Portable restaurants park along streets and sidewalks with tempting displays of sandwiches, sweets and soft drinks.

head or some unrecognizable object considered a delicacy will appear on your plate. If you can eat it with a smile of pleasure, your host will be delighted. If not, politely insist that the honor be his and place it on his plate. If you can eat what is offered without bothering to find out what you are eating, you are in for some very pleasant surprises in delicious food. As time passes, you will find yourself preferring the Oriental food to Western dishes.

Eating out in Vietnam at the better restaurants is very expensive. The decor of a restaurant offers little indication of the quality of its food. Some of the finest food I have eaten in the Orient has been at out-of-the-way restaurants that by United States standards would be considered "shacks," with sanitary conditions that leave much to be desired.

The bowls and utensils are washed in cold, soapless water and must have the grease wiped off with a piece of paper provided for that purpose. On one occasion the waiter picked up a set of used chopsticks from another table, wiped them off with a rag and handed them to us for use. You know you are asking for a bad case of stomach trouble, tuberculosis or hepatitis by eating the food in such a place. Despite the miserable conditions, the Vietnamese fill the tables to capacity. You may have been invited here by a Vietnamese friend whom you do not want to offend. You can be assured that if your friend brought you here, the food will be excellent, far superior to the clean, sanitary establishments normally catering to tourists.

Very good restaurants with excellent food and sanitary conditions can be found in the larger cities. Among these, the French establishments can usually be counted on to excel. Snails boiled with butter and garlic, thick soups served with huge chunks of French bread, superbly flavored seafoods and vintage wines are a match in quality to that found anywhere. Excellent Chinese food is also served in many establishments, but for the very choicest top quality Vietnamese food, you will have to either be invited

Santa Claus, Rudolph the Red-Nosed Reindeer and Batman in the form of plastic inflated toys are on sale in the marketplace.

to a Vietnamese home or take your chances in less than favorable surroundings. For some reason, the restaurants with Westernized accommodations and conditions seldom feature really fine Vietnamese food.

Such succulent dishes as sweet and sour pork, fried rice, shark fin soup, corn-crab soup, seafoods and plump rice birds will haunt your fondest memories for years after leaving Vietnam.

Join a Vietnamese friend for a bottle of soda and it will usually be served warm with a large glassful of ice. Your friend will probably order large, fluffy fried chips made from rice that look like giant potato chips. He may also order a few sun-dried, tough as leather, squid. The waiter will pound or chop the squid, then heat it over an open alcohol flame. Chunks are torn off and chewed as you drink. You will probably develop a taste for the mild-flavored squid and begin ordering it yourself if your friend doesn't.

If you are invited to a Vietnamese home for dinner, you will probably be greeted by and introduced to the family when you arrive. If you are a man, the wife and children will not join you for dinner. You will eat with your host and perhaps a few of his male friends. Your friend's wife or a servant will serve the dinner while the little children peek around corners to watch, but stay out of the way. If one of the guests is a woman, the wife of the host will some-

Ping-Pong is a major event. This athlete was high-point man with a gold medal and two trophies.

times join the guests at the table; otherwise the men eat alone.

Chicken or duck will most likely be one of the foods served. In a traditional household, the coagulated blood of the bird, sprinkled with crushed peanuts, will be served in a bowl. You can politely refuse this delicacy. Many Vietnamese also do not care for it. Your host has included the blood on the menu to show you that the bird was freshly killed in your honor.

It is considered polite to bring candy or some small treat for your host to give to his children. A mother or father of your host may also be living in the household. Be sure to greet them politely with a slight nod of the head when you arrive and leave.

Never offer to shake hands with a Vietnamese woman. If she has become accustomed to Western ways, she will offer her hand for you to shake. If not, she will be embarrassed by your offer.

Tropical fruits of many kinds are readily available. Bananas in several sizes and flavors are available in most markets. My favorite is not much bigger than your thumb and has a strawberrylike flavor.

Custard apples about the size of a baseball are a light green on the lumpy outside and white inside. The inside is soft and delicious.

Other fruits come in several sizes and shapes. Some look like a red egg with many soft spines sticking out. For want of the real name, we called them

A gold medal for first place in cross-country cycling.

porcupine eggs. Durian fruit is a large fruit sometimes weighing more than ten pounds. The outside is tough and bristly and the inside a bright yellow with large pecan-sized and shaped seeds. This fruit smells terrible, but tastes very good. Most fruits found in the United States can be bought in the large marketplaces in the cities, but because most temperate climate fruits such as pears, apples and grapes do not grow well in Vietnam, they must be imported at high cost.

Vietnam's 1650 miles of seashore offer a variety of activities. Unfortunately, accommodations for enjoying the seashore are not usually available. Many miles of excellent beaches are seldom used for bathing, for the Vietnamese do not seem to be fond of swimming. Young children are often seen playing in the shallows, but few adults participate. In many areas the coastal waters are crystal clear with an abundance of underwater plant and animal life, offering an opportunity for unspoiled skin diving. Future development of this natural resource is sure to come. Hawaii has little to offer that cannot be equalled or surpassed by Vietnam when it comes to quality and beauty in beaches or scenery.

Western types of fishing tackle are not usually available. The hundreds of varieties of fish in large quantities could provide the basis for future development of sport fishing for tourists. The Vietnamese regard fishing as a means of getting food and consider it a foolish waste of effort for someone who can afford to pay for fish in the market. Fishing boats can be rented for the day if you provide your own tackle and bait and can convince the boat owner that you sincerely want to catch your own fish.

During times of peace, Vietnam was considered to be one of the world's finest areas for big game hunting. Buffalo, deer, tiger, elephant and many other species offered a wide selection of trophies. At present, due to the war, hunting is out of the question.

Vietnam has much to offer to the tourist who is adventurous and can find the patience and courage to cope with the presently existing conditions. Given a peacetime economy, it is sure to develop as one of the world's choice resort areas.

Chapter VII

EDUCATION—THE KEY TO PROGRESS

"Education has always been held in high regard in Vietnamese society. The traditional reverence for the scholar in ancient times and the high esteem reserved for the intellectuals in the French tradition, both have contributed to this respect for learning. To most Vietnamese, urban as well as rural, education represents the essential steppingstone to social and financial success."*

In the early days of the present conflict in Vietnam, the public schools were regarded by the Viet Cong as an arm of the Saigon government and a threat to their cause because of the progovernment teaching that took place in the schools. As a result, hundreds of schools were destroyed and teachers were often abducted or assassinated.

---

*An Introduction to Vietnam, Second Edition (Saigon: The Vietnam Council on Foreign Relations, 1969).

Hamlet schools often suffer severe damage during attacks.

During the writer's stay in Binh Thuan Province, one hamlet school was destroyed and rebuilt for the seventh time. The intense Vietnamese drive to secure an education for their children resulted in an adverse effect for the aims of the Viet Cong.

Students seldom missed school even though threats against their lives were often made. When schools were blown up, tents or the open air served as a classroom while parents pooled their resources to rebuild the schools. When the teacher was killed or abducted, anyone who could read and write took her place as the teacher. Only in areas controlled

Temporary shelters replace schools destroyed by the war.

exclusively by the Viet Cong were they successful in keeping the schools closed. The end result of their efforts was to strengthen the hostility toward the Viet Cong in areas where the people were progovernment. In areas under their control, their own supporters' children were deprived of an education.

In 1969, the Viet Cong changed their policy toward the schools due to the negative results of their former efforts. Since then, the schools and the teachers have had considerably less problems with Viet Cong action.

A new teacher volunteers for a hazardous position in a remote hamlet.

When the country was divided in 1954, South Vietnam had no universities, no teachers' colleges, no medical schools and few technical schools. North Vietnam had been the center of educational development and access to those schools no longer existed for South Vietnamese. In 1954, only 16% of the school-age population were able to attend school.

The French did not appear to be interested in educating the majority of the Vietnamese people. They provided only enough schools to train the number of Vietnamese they felt were essential for filling positions in government that they considered too low in rank to be held by Frenchmen. Fortunately, the government of South Vietnam realized that education was essential to progress and proceeded to fill this need.

The number of elementary school classrooms rose from 8,191 in 1954 to 41,604 in 1969. In 1954, only 16% of the children ages 6 through 11 attended school. In 1972, 94% of the children this age attended school. During the same period, high school enrollment rose from 3% to 23%. This increase in education in a country engaged in an active war is nothing short of spectacular.

In 1972, seven universities with over 41,000 students, five teachers' colleges, a medical school, dental schools, and many agricultural and technical schools were in full operation in South Vietnam where none had existed in 1954.

School construction carries high priority. Hundreds of new schools are built each year.

An impressive ceremony is held for the dedication of a new school.

Statistics, however, do not tell the full story and they overlook basic facts that are necessary for a clear understanding of the situation that exists.

Elementary enrollment has risen from 400,865 students in 1954 to over 2.7 million in 1972. Secondary enrollment has risen from 53,501 students in 1954 to 710,000 in 1972. It must be kept in mind that these figures represent enrollment in both public and private schools.

Elementary age children have far greater opportunity to enter public schools than do secondary students. Of eligible students, 68% are able to enter public elementary schools, but only 6% of secondary age students have this opportunity. In 1968, 3500 elementary graduates applied for a public secondary education in Binh Thuan Province. Of these, only 365 were admitted to the public high school; the balance competed for entry in private high schools where an additional 2000 were accommodated. This shortage of secondary facilities is further aggravated by the lack of quality in the education of the elementary school graduates, many of whom are not able to qualify by passing the rigid entrance exams.

Of the 552,000 students enrolled in secondary schools in 1968-69, only 35% attended public high schools.

Most private schools are organized by religious groups with the Buddhist and Catholic schools being the most common. The balance are organized on a

An American educator takes part in a 90-day training session for rural school teachers.

tuition, profit-making basis and are usually considered as less desirable in quality.

The Ministry of Education in Saigon is in direct control of all public schools in Vietnam. The ministry makes all major decisions concerning education, controls all budgets, curriculums, teacher training, teacher certification and salaries, and publishes the standardized tests that are required for secondary entrance and graduation. Private school students must meet the same standards as public school students in order to graduate.

Vietnamese schools still adhere to the French system of education.

Students begin school at grade 5 and progress to grade 1, which is equivalent to the United States grade 5. It is necessary to pass an entrance exam to enter the First Cycle (Bac I). First Cycle consists of grades 7, 6, 5, 4, which are equivalent to U. S. grades 6, 7, 8, 9. Since 1966, an examination is no longer required for completion of the First Cycle and students are allowed to enter the Second Cycle (Bac II), grades 3, 2, 1 (U. S. 10, 11, 12), without further testing.

For most students the certificate at the completion of elementary school or the diploma at the end of the First Cycle will signify the end of their schooling. The shortage of secondary schools and the high cost of private schools or the lack of ability to pass

111

Graduation day for much-needed elementary teachers. American and Vietnamese officials take part in the ceremony.

entrance exams will result in the termination of their education.

The thousands of children in refugee settlements face an even greater obstacle to advanced education. Most refugee schools only include grades 5, 4, and 3 of the elementary school. Students are often unable to enroll in another school for grades 2 and 1 and are therefore unable to progress further than the first three years of schooling offered in the refugee settlements.

The word "shortage" describes most aspects of public education in Vietnam. A shortage of classrooms, a shortage of teachers, a shortage of textbooks, a shortage of funds, and other shortages of all kinds act as a deterrent to progress.

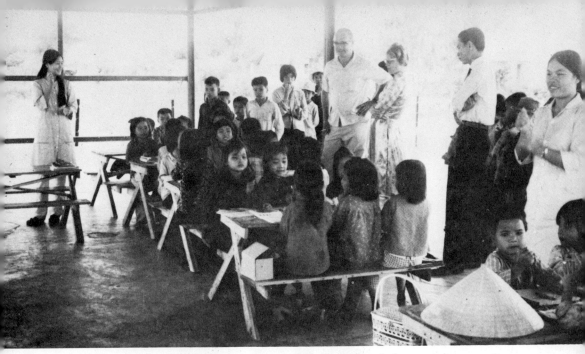

An experimental kindergarten class in an open-air shelter receives great praise from students and parents.

Classrooms are built according to national plans. Schools are allocated a specific number of bags of cement, sheets of roofing and funds to complete classrooms and furnish them. Modifications of the plans are allowed only in the manner of decorations. This standardization has resulted in tremendous savings in construction costs and a resultant increase in the number of new classrooms.

The opening of a new school or even the completion of new classrooms is considered as an occasion for great ceremony. The village notables are seated in a place of honor dressed in black jackets, white pants and a special black hat to show their rank. Special places are also reserved for the village council, the older women, the hamlet officials, the district chief and his staff and perhaps even the province

113

High school girls pedal bicycles to school. Their white "Ao Dai" is the traditional costume for high school girls throughout Vietnam.

chief, who is sure to be accompanied by many soldiers and government officials.

Palm leaves are braided into green arches and a table is placed near the speakers' lectern for a vase with a bouquet of flowers.

The students stand in their school uniforms in neat rows, each carrying a small yellow and red flag of South Vietnam.

The speeches go on and on; one after another official must be given the opportunity to speak. Everyone listens politely and seems to enjoy the pro-

114

longed ceremony. Only the children betray their restlessness by a shifting of weight from one foot to the other or by staring intently at the fly seated on their classmate's shoulder. In spite of restlessness, they maintain perfect discipline throughout the ceremony.

A severe shortage of teachers exists. Teacher training facilities have not been able to keep pace with the rapid building of new schools. As an emergency measure, the Ministry of Education is issuing teaching certificates to high school graduates who have completed a 90-day teacher training course.

The average salary of a rural elementary school teacher is about $30 a month. Inflation has made it very difficult to live on this amount. The low salary, poor working conditions and the lure of better pay at private schools or of up to $300 a month working for Americans has led many to leave the hardships and hazards of rural public schools.

Most teachers, however, remain true to their profession in spite of hardships. Though their salary is small, their prestige is great and they are highly respected in their communities and by their students.

When a teacher enters a classroom, the students all rise and solemnly greet her. They remain standing until given permission to be seated. Truancy is almost unheard of in the elementary school and the threat of being sent home in disgrace is fearful

Elementary students in Saigon wait for a school bus.

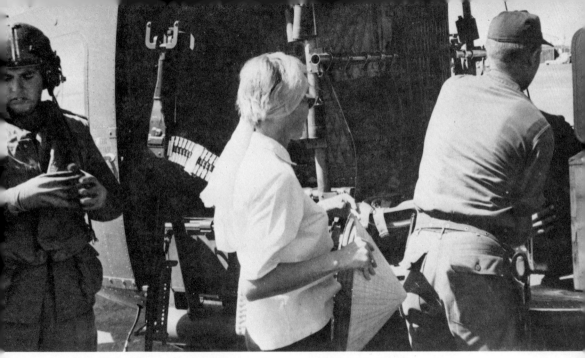

Teachers and supplies must be transported by helicopter to some remote areas.

enough to encourage good behavior from even the most restless students.

Secondary school students are not required to attend class if they do not wish to. They may choose instead to share notes with a friend who did attend or attend only when a subject that is unclear to them is being explained. All that is necessary is that they pass the final exams at the end of the term.

The schools in Vietnam do not have athletic teams. Education is considered a very serious matter. Students will often form their own teams after school and some interschool competition does take place, always accompanied by large crowds of spectators.

A young American, Rick Swiegert, worked in Binh Thuan province for the International Voluntary Service. During his two years, Rick organized many soccer teams and encouraged the people to build over two dozen new soccer fields.

Rick worked primarily in a remote rural area with a population composed mostly of Chams, Nungs and Montagnards.

One of his many achievements was the organization of a three-day campout weekend for over six hundred school children. Arranging for food, transportation, tents and organizing three days of continuous activity was no small task. Though he did most of the organizing, Rick managed to stay in the background and let the people and students feel that they themselves had accomplished the organization.

The area where the campout was held was an active combat area with almost nightly small-scale engagements. Everyone was a bit uneasy about the children's safety during the three days, but no unpleasant incidents took place.

Every Boy Scout troop, 4T group, Campfire Girl troop and school took part in the program. Athletic events, dancing contests, demonstrations and dozens of other activities made the affair a truly memorable one for all who took part.

Teen-agers in Vietnam enjoy fun and games like teen-agers everywhere. Though they work and play hard, they seldom forget their manners and always show respect for their teachers, parents and adults.

A weekend campout with competitive sports, school demonstrations and a talent contest provide the highlights of the year's activities.

While working in Vietnam, the writer employed a college student as an interpreter. He was studying to be a teacher and quit his job when the school vacation was over. When asked why he was quitting to go back to college when he was receiving $150 a month as an interpreter and would receive only $30 a month as a teacher, he replied, "I appreciate the money I am earning here, but my country needs teachers badly. Education for our people is our only hope for the future and in this way I can contribute the most."

Students in school uniforms demonstrate a folk dance.

Our hearts were filled with sadness to learn that he had been captured and executed by the Viet Cong at Hue during the 1968 Tet offensive. His life was forfeited for the unforgivable crime of having worked for the Americans.

In 1968, a major battle took place in Binh Thuan province. Forty-four thousand refugees swarmed into the small capital city of Phan Thiet.

In a short time hundreds of volunteers helped them erect temporary tents and shelters and supplied food and water. The teen-agers played a prominent part in these acts of kindness. The Boy Scouts set up a tent camp in a vacant lot and for several months, until the people were able to return home, provided for them. Twenty-four hours a day Boy Scouts were on duty supplying first aid, water, collecting garbage and making life more comfortable for the people. As the people began returning home, they cared for the children during the day while their parents and older children rebuilt their homes.

Two high school boys, all on their own, scrounged a huge army tent, collected ammunition boxes for desks and set up a school for about a hundred young children. Without pay of any kind, they conducted school every day for nearly six months until the children returned to their homes and their own schools.

Textbooks and other classroom supplies are also a problem. Often the teacher is the only one with a book and must read everything out loud to the class. Until recently, teachers wrote their own textbooks and sold them to the students. A particularly good text would often be published and sold at bookstores. Uniformity of instruction did not exist. In response to this difficulty the United States educational advisors and the Vietnamese Ministry of Education cooperatively wrote textbooks for the elementary grades and published fourteen million for distribution. Poor planning and distribution methods resulted in a loss of millions of these books before they reached the classrooms.

Cham schoolgirls perform an ancient fan dance.

Education in Vietnam is largely based on rote learning with the student memorizing most of the material covered in order to pass his examinations. This method of teaching does a poor job of developing creativity and qualities of leadership. American influence has resulted in a shift to a more current approach to teaching methods.

Mr. Loan, chief of education in Binh Thuan province, had spent a few months in the United States on a study tour of U. S. elementary schools. His experience has led him to become quite Westernized in his approach and this is evident in the quality of the local schools.

The funds used to send him and others on that tour were well spent. He is a capable and progressive educational leader.

The writer attended many of his monthly teachers' meetings and inservice training programs. The exchange of ideas and updating of methods were enjoyed and of benefit to all attending. Many school systems in the U. S. could profit from Mr. Loan's good example.

Mr. Loan is one of the forty-nine chiefs of education located in the forty-four provinces and five autonomous cities. His duties consist of supervision of the elementary schools in the province.

Theoretically the high schools are under the supervision of the principal of the largest public secondary school in each province. This principal receives no additional pay for serving in this capacity and has little or no authority in schools other than his own. As a result, he does little other than conduct the business of his own school.

Plans are under way to give overall authority for both elementary schools and secondary schools to either the high school principal or the present chief of education. It would seem that the chief of education would be the logical choice, but he seldom has a college degree, while the high school principal does. Therefore, considerable discussion is taking place over who should control.

Despite the many problems still to be solved, South Vietnam can be justifiably proud of its accomplishments in education. The tremendous achievements of the past sixteen years are a positive sign of sincerity of purpose and true nation building.

Chapter VIII

HIGHLIGHTS OF VIETNAM

The diversity in climate and terrain have created a situation in which it is necessary to travel throughout the country in order to truly be able to say "I have seen Vietnam." The tense situation that exists due to the political situation severely limits advisable travel.

The delta, the seashore and the mountains represent three very different areas, each presenting its own unique "look" at Vietnam.

Can Tho, in the heart of the delta, is situated in an area that is readily accessible from Saigon by bus, which is not recommended; by car, which is difficult to arrange, and by Air Vietnam, which is the best choice for travel anywhere in the country.

Can Tho and the immediately surrounding country offers a good example of life in the delta area. Here life goes on as it has for hundreds of years. The war, with its restrictions on freedom of movement, is in evidence, but in most respects Can Tho

The mighty Mekong River, lifeline of the delta region.

A thatched roof with walls of mud and straw plastered over woven branches provides a home for a typical rice-farming family.

remains a center of marketing for the people of the surrounding area. Hotel accommodations are adequate but simple, and local travel is limited to walking or by cycle. The pace of life is leisurely as compared to the more rapid pace in Saigon.

A brief stop at the local United States Agency for International Development office will provide you with information about local points of interest. If you plan to travel in the countryside, the stop is an absolute necessity to provide a measure of safety in the present situation.

This office is staffed by U. S. civilian and military personnel for purposes other than serving as a tourist information center. In all probability, the men will be working long hours and under difficult situations. Tact on your part is a necessity when seeking assistance and, if successful, could produce an invitation for side trips into areas otherwise impossible to see.

A trip to the mountains means a trip to Dalat, the only fairly secure mountainous area readily available to tourists via Air Vietnam. Dalat has been noted as a vacation and resort center for those seeking to escape the heat of the lowland areas. Most accommodations and conveniences of a resort area are available here. Good hotels, excellent dining, fair entertainment and fabulous scenery abound for a price. Dalat is the vegetable capital of Vietnam. Hundreds of hectares are devoted to the production

Endless channels and small boats provide the only means of transportation in some areas of the Mekong Delta. Electric power lines provide evidence of economic progress.

of lettuce, strawberries and other crops that will not grow well in the more tropical lowland climate. The temperature in the evening drops to the point of requiring warmer clothing and blankets for sleeping.

An interesting side trip to Duc Tho when the security situation permits, will provide a look at the work that "man's humanity to man" can invoke. A young American doctor, Dr. Jim Turpin of California, has built a hospital complex staffed by personnel from as many as twenty-three different countries. They serve at subsistence pay, devoting their

Fishing nets, raised and lowered by a hand-operated windlass, provide small fish for a family's table.

time and energy to making life a little more bearable to the often impoverished mountain people of the area by providing free medical and nutritional aid to those who need it. Dr. Turpin has also established clinics on two houseboats in Hong Kong, administering to the "boat people" in Aberdeen Harbor. If you are fortunate enough to find him at the clinic, you will be able to meet an individual who will, without any doubt, greatly impress you and probably convince you that service to humanity is indeed the best work of life.

A short flight north brings you to the ancient capital city of Hue. Hue is an autonomous city, oper-

"Project Concern" begun by Dr. Jim Turpin of California, U.S.A., provides medical aid for thousands in Hong Kong and Vietnam through the voluntary services of personnel from twenty-three countries.

ating with its own government which answers directly to the Saigon government and not to the provincial authorities. The university, the ancient citadel with its statuary and unique construction, the beautiful Perfume River and other sights make this an interesting city to visit. Tourist accommodations and personal security are not the best and until the situation changes considerably Hue should probably be avoided unless special advanced arrangements are made.

The seashore offers a variety of lifestyles and points of interest. Da Nang offers a look at life in the

434

C47 cargo planes of World War II still provide safe, dependable service and are often the only means of transportation available to remote areas.

oldest deep-water harbor in Vietnam. The dock area is a bustling hum of activity. Small boats and huge ocean-going vessels line the docks to load and unload their cargoes. The city itself offers adequate accommodations and some choice dining areas. Restrictions on military personnel in the area have resulted in a more subdued night life than that found in Saigon. Many historical points of interest are readily available to the student of the culture of Vietnam. Excellent stone carvings from the marble mountain area are available at bargain prices in some of the local shops.

Farther south, the city of Na Trang offers a more leisurely atmosphere and a time for relaxation. Several miles of excellent beach complete with outdoor cafes provide a welcome break in the schedule of the busy tourist. A small fishing village south of the beach area has boats for rent that can take you to the off-shore islands with crystal-clear waters for some choice skin diving and shell collecting. Shops and stands in the boat rental area offer rare seashells and shell jewelry at near giveaway prices to the individual who is willing to spend some time bargaining.

In the same area is located one of the finest oceanography centers in all of Southeast Asia. The hours open to the public vary, but the inconvenience in timing that may result is worth the effort for a tour. Near the center, overlooking the bay, is a French restaurant with choicely prepared seafood. Huge lobsters broiled in butter are their specialty. Another restaurant known as "Fergaut's" is also a necessary stop. Their "Coquilles de Saint Jacques," a mixture of seafoods baked in rich cheese sauce in the shell of a half clam, is a culinary delight that will bring back pleasant memories. Carved seashell lamps can be found in the small shops in the downtown area that are truly works of art.

The hotel Na Trang offers good accommodations, fair food and occasional entertainment. A nearby Chinese restaurant features an extensive menu of well-prepared food at a reasonable price.

Camranh Bay, located about seventy-five miles farther south, is a marvel of engineering skill. Hundreds of acres of storage facilities, dock sites and airstrips were virtually carved out of the mountains

132

Military helicopters can land anywhere, but are only available for high-priority projects.

and sand dunes in the area, creating a new deep-water harbor and one of the finest airfields in Southeast Asia. Tourist accommodations are poor and are not advisable.

Proceeding south, Phan Rang is of interest to the archaeologist, as the location of the best existing remnants of the Champa Empire. Ancient ruins can be seen on the surrounding hillsides. Very little effort has been made at excavation or preservation. Phan Rang has a medium-sized U. S. air base and a USAID office. Tourist accommodations are poor and a stop at USAID offices is advisable.

133

A typical home in a small fishing village along the coast.

A good look at an agricultural-fishing community is provided by a stop at Phan Thiet while en route south to Saigon. Overnight accommodations are available but can be considered poor. A stop at USAID headquarters is a necessity for security reasons.

Local "Nuc Mum" factories permeate the air with an odor of fermenting fish. This fish sauce is produced in over two hundred small local plants with a total production of over a million liters a year, making Phan Thiet the "Nuc Mum" capital of Vietnam. This sauce is made by placing alternate layers of fish and salt in huge vats and fermenting for six months to a year. The juice is then drained and diluted with water. Vietnamese use this sauce much as we use catsup. Once you develop a taste for it, your food seems to lack flavor without it.

The Qung Hung goldsmithing shop operated by Mr. Tu Tu offers examples of the goldsmithing art that are representative of a skill that is rapidly becoming a lost art. Watchbands containing over three hundred individually fitted and soldered pieces are available at bargain prices. Meeting the amiable proprietor Mr. Tu Tu is reason enough for a visit to his shop. Should you be fortunate enough to receive a dinner invitation to sample his cooking, you will have a meal that is far superior to any you might have in Vietnam's finest restaurants.

A fine beach and further examples of ancient Cham architecture are also found here at Phan Thiet.

The Moon Mong River joins the sea at Phan Thiet, capital of Binh Thuan Province.

Boats of the Phan Thiet fishing fleet lie at anchor waiting for the tide to carry them out to sea.

Vung Tau is located farther south along the coast due east of Saigon. It has been considered the outstanding seaside resort by the wealthy of Vietnam for many years. The influx of large numbers of military personnel has resulted in the development of a more Westernized tourist exploitation atmosphere. An abundance of night clubs and other establishments designed to make money represent a departure from the typical Vietnamese style of living.

Sun-drenched beaches, modern accommodations and a freedom from the fears of the war continue to draw crowds of people each weekend. Vung Tau may someday serve as an alternative to a trip to the French Riviera or to Hawaii.

Your tour of Vietnam undoubtedly began at the Ton Son Nhut airfield in Saigon. Saigon, the sprawling giant of a city, has much to offer and deserves a chapter of its own on our tour of Vietnam.

Chapter IX

SAIGON—PARIS OF THE ORIENT

Saigon, the capital city of South Vietnam, has often been called the Paris of the Orient. Its 2.2 million inhabitants make it one of the largest cities in Southeast Asia.

The wide tree-lined boulevards and French architecture do indeed remind one of Paris. Unlike most Oriental cities, Saigon seems to move at a more leisurely pace. The streets are crowded with traffic and people are everywhere, but the general atmosphere fails to indicate the sense of urgency found in Tokyo, Bangkok or Hong Kong.

The lack of funds for effective city management is also readily apparent in the form of piles of foul-smelling garbage and littered streets. The once-beautiful city has lost some of its Parisian splendor. The war has left its scars in the form of bullet-marked walls and fences along the streets near Ton Son Nhut airport. Everywhere one sees armed soldiers, police,

Rooftops of Saigon give evidence of the dense population below.

barbed wire, protective screening and sand-bag barricades.

The city is bursting at the seams with Vietnamese that have left the country to find jobs in the city or to escape the threat of the war.

The government has made noble efforts to clean up the city and restore it to order, but the staggering numbers of people make the job nearly impossible. For a time the government appears to make progress and the garbage disappears and order seems to be on its way, only to have the process again reverse itself due to lack of funds or labor disputes.

In spite of the many problems, the spirit of the city seems to be indestructible and survives all manner of abuse.

Wide boulevards and circular fountain in downtown Saigon are products of French engineering.

Reports of terrorist activities dampen the spirits of adventure in most tourists when they first arrive in Saigon, but the enchantment of the Orient soon wins out and caution is thrown to the winds. There is much to see and much to do and the vastly over-exaggerated hazards lose out to the charm of the city.

A good place to begin your tour of the city is the open-air patio cafe of the Continental Hotel. Here one can leisurely enjoy a cool drink and watch the activities of the day. Peddlers with their wares have set up shop on the sidewalks along the boulevards. In places, it is necessary to walk single file or walk in the street to get around their display goods. Some

141

The Lower House Building in front of Lam Son Square.

of the more permanent have built small stands with canvas roofs; others have only the bare sidewalk.

"Let the buyer beware" is an old slogan that definitely applies here. The sidewalk peddlers sell almost anything: wood carvings, artwork, tools, food, American whisky and black market items. Their prices are usually reasonable and many good buys can be made if one knows the local prices and can determine the quality of the goods. Many peddlers will quote prices that are much too high in hope of making extra money. A shrewd buyer can usually bring the price down. The appearance of the mer-

The new modern presidential palace in Saigon is a striking testimony to the progressive spirit of the people and their struggle to maintain economic independence among the nations of the world.

French architecture is exhibited in the design of this government office building.

chandise does not always tell the true value. Labels are often changed to trick the unwary buyer. More than one young soldier has been disappointed to find that the baby leopard he bought was really a yellow alley cat with shoe polish spots.

Beware also of the little girls with the paper cones of peanuts for sale. Let them crowd around you and your watch or wallet may soon be gone.

Unfortunately, the writer finds himself guilty of the same offense he has criticized other writers of. Time and again the tourist is warned of the many thieves that are eager to rob him of his money, regardless of which country he may be in. The fact of the matter is that the vast majority of the peddlers and shopkeepers are honest people trying to make an honest living. Only a few are trying to cheat you. In Asian and Latin American countries it is customary to ask a higher price than is really wanted in order to let the buyer bargain for a lower price. The buyer can leave feeling he has received a shrewd bargain and the shopkeeper has received the price he wanted. On more than one occasion I have had peddlers or shopkeepers send a small child hurrying after me to inform me that I had left a package or had not received enough change.

Some very fine bargains can be made in the shops near Tu Do Street. Artwork, especially oil paintings, can be found that are painted by some of the finest artists in Vietnam and are on sale for $25 to $50 each.

Flower stand in the Central Market.

These are often one of a kind paintings depicting all facets of Vietnamese life and are painted with painstaking care and a master's hand.

Silver and gold jewelry, small ancient jade pins and pendants, and ivory carvings are higher in price than in Bangkok or Hong Kong, but due to the skilled craftsmanship and unique Vietnamese characteristics, are bargains nonetheless. Who can place a value on a delicately carved jade flower or bird that is hundreds of years old and one of a kind? It is worth what the buyer is willing to pay and the seller willing

Pony carts from the country haul produce to market.

to take to part with it. A true lover of old jade will receive full value in hours of fondling and gazing at the work of art just as a sports car lover receives a satisfaction from polishing his metal masterpiece.

Fans, combs and pins made of sea tortoise shell inlaid with mother-of-pearl are on sale in many shops and represent a good example of Vietnamese handicraft.

Ceramics are a joy and beauty to behold. Huge elephants weighing sixty pounds each, temple dogs, delicate multicolored vases, children's banks and dozens of other items done with a skill and technique seldom found elsewhere are on sale in the shops along Tu Do Street. The connoisseur of ceramics will be in his glory among the many superb pieces that are offered for sale at low prices.

Leather goods in the form of wallets, golf bags, handbags and handmade shoes are to be found at prices much below those in the United States for items of similar quality.

The tailor-made shoes will take a week or two before they are ready, but they are well worth the inconvenience of the extra time. The writer has worn a pair of the elephant hide shoes for over two years almost daily, with little sign of wear other than the need for occasional resoling. They require no break-in period and feel like old friends from the day they are purchased.

Three souvenir items that are an absolute must for the female tourist are the beautiful, feminine "Ao Dai" the national costume worn by the women on all occasions, the souvenir dolls dressed in Ao Dai and the cone-shaped hat called a "Non La."

In Saigon, as in most places in Vietnam, the men have adopted Western clothing. The white shirt is a status symbol and few educated men would be seen without one. In even the remotest villages, men of means or public office wear white shirts to meetings and social affairs. In Saigon, women are seen wearing Western clothing, but even here they are few in

The market is a busy place filled with strange odors and much to see.

number. The Ao Dai is still the prominent wearing apparel for the well-dressed woman.

Modern Westernized hotel accommodations are available in Saigon with good food and fair service.

Among these the Continental, the Majestique, Embassy, Oscar, and Excelsior are the favorites of Westerners. Be prepared to pay exorbitant prices. The wartime economy and influx of Westerners on expense accounts have caused prices at these establishments to skyrocket.

Vietnam is seldom considered as a tourist haven, yet the tourist bureau claims 44,000 tourists visited the country in 1967 and the number has rapidly increased. With most of the better hotels nearly filled with semipermanent guests, it would be a good idea to reserve a room well in advance of your arrival.

Traffic in Saigon flows at a steady pace with streets much too crowded at peak hours to even think about hurrying. Most traffic consists of bicycles, cyclos, taxis and trucks. Occasional pony carts and man-drawn vehicles are also observed. A few private automobiles are seen, but are not common. Most travel is done by taxis and cyclos. The taxis are small French vehicles twenty or thirty years old and in various stages of repair. Somehow they manage to keep running effectively year after year. Forget about the meter in your taxi. The law requires the driver to use the meter, but it is not enforced. Inflation has made it impossible to operate the vehicles at the meter prices. Taxi fares are reasonable, but you must agree on a price before getting in or you may find yourself being greatly overcharged by one of the less honest drivers who will scream at the top of his lungs until you pay his price.

Riding in a cyclo is an unforgettable experience recommended only for the stout of heart. Cyclos are like a bicycle or a motorcycle with two wheels up front with a seat between them for the passenger. The drivers delight in weaving in and out of traffic and depending on a split-second timing to keep from getting hit by trucks and other vehicles. When you

Small stores carry a variety of goods.

are sitting up front acting as a front bumper, the experience can be somewhat startling.

In 1967, the streets were crowded with motorbikes and motorcycles driven by young men referred to as "Saigon cowboys." Hundreds of them were parked along the boulevards in the evening. The young men who drove them were usually listed as students at schools in Saigon and were therefore exempt from going into the army. Most of them did not attend classes and went to the school only to pay their tuition. Changes in the draft laws ended

Sidewalk stands often have good bargains and "black market" goods.

their student deferments and by 1969 the streets were noticeably free from their presence. The army of Vietnam had increased its manpower by 50 percent.

Moving along with the traffic, one can often see the small pony carts filled to overflowing with farm products and families in from the country. The enormous loads that are pulled by these small ponies, apparently without much effort, is amazing.

Within easy walking distance from the Continental Hotel in central Saigon is the wide boulevard

Nguyen Hue with its many peddlers and beautiful flower stands and gift shops. At the end of the boulevard is the Saigon River that has made Saigon one of the busiest seaports in the world. This is a poor area to be in after dark, but is perfectly safe in the daytime.

For a few piasters one can rent a small motorized boat and ride along the waterfront past the many ocean-going vessels as they unload their wares from the far corners of the earth.

A floating restaurant on the Saigon River at the end of Nguyen Hue Street is world-famous for its excellent seafood. A number of bombings by terrorists at this restaurant has cut down severely on its volume of business.

Out in the harbor and along the riverbanks for miles are thousands of small boats that serve as homes for the river people who make a living by hauling freight or selling to the larger vessels. Whole families are crowded into the cramped quarters of the smaller vessels, leaving little room for cargo. Many of the river people live on their boats and work in Saigon during the day.

A short way from the floating restaurant is an area of specialized shops selling plants and animals of all kinds. Monkeys, snakes, birds, cats, puppies, rabbits and a multitude of potted plants make this an interesting area to visit.

Racks of cooked chickens, ducks and pigeons lure shoppers with their succulent odors.

Cyclos provide a thrilling ride, with the passenger up front feeling like a human bumper.

For those who enjoy modern architecture, the Presidential palace and the new United States Embassy are worth seeing. They are impressive structures, especially the palace surrounded by its broad expanse of gardens and lawn. Numerous guards prevent the tourist from entering the place except on special occasions.

The "Nha Ta De Saigon" Catholic cathedral is also a place of interest. In front of the cathedral is a large statue of the Virgin Mary erected and dedicated in memory of the former U. S. President John F. Kennedy.

The National Museum in Saigon contains fine examples of Vietnamese art and archaeological discoveries. Among the artifacts are the large bronze drums that have led archaeologists to believe that Vietnamese had been a part of the Malayan-Polynesian culture in ancient times.

The Saigon zoo was and may still be the finest in the Orient. At present, financial difficulties have caused a reduction in its former excellence.

Cholon, the neighboring city of Saigon, borders on Saigon and it is difficult to determine where one begins and the other ends.

The city is composed mostly of Chinese. One is reminded of Hong Kong by the many signs written in the Chinese language. Shopping here is excellent, but frequent terrorist activity makes this an ill-advised area for tourists, particularly after dark.

Huge baskets of oranges and other fruit are tempting to a small boy. It is better not to look when one has no money.

Gasoline engines are fitted with long shafts and propellers to make effective outboard motors.

Waterfront markets offer an assortment of monkeys, birds, cats, dogs and other pets.

As night falls on Saigon the activity in the streets changes and many of the sidewalk peddlers gather up their wares for the day. The people in the streets are mostly the younger crowd on their way to the many movie theaters and restaurants.

Night clubs are plentiful, particularly on Tu Do Street. The music is Westernized, the many hostesses wear Western clothing and the prices are exorbitant. Few Vietnamese frequent the clubs on Tu Do Street. The tourist prices are out of reach of their income.

Your Vietnamese friends can escort you to night clubs that are seldom visited by Westerners and offer

International House operated exclusively for Americans and their guests. Dining and music for dancing are featured nightly.

good Vietnamese music and reasonable prices. In some of these clubs you will feel like an invader infringing upon the privacy of the local residents. In others you will be welcomed, particularly if you are accompanied by a Vietnamese.

Eleven o'clock arrives and the curfew is on. The streets have cleared and except for a few stray taxis, cyclos, and Vietnamese hurrying home, are quite empty of the masses of humanity that fill them during the day.

Police and soldiers standing guard at regular intervals are the only signs of life. The city is asleep.

If you are staying at one of the more modern hotels, your night need not end. The rooftop terraces are still open. Sitting at your table overlooking the city, you can see the aircraft arriving and leaving the distant Ton Son Nhut Airfield. Groups of helicopters hurry by on night operations. The distant booming of artillery is ever present. The sky in the distance is lighted by parachute flares that light the ground while helicopters seek out the Viet Cong. On occasion you will see the red flow of mini-gunfire from the helicopters hosing the earth with their messages of death as they catch the enemy in the open rice fields outside the city.

One wonders where it will all end. When will man end his inhumanity to man? When will these warmhearted, courageous people again find peace in their ravaged land?

Vietnamese girls train to help villagers and provide security.

Chapter X

THE BUILDING OF A NATION

A new nation is being built in South Vietnam, a nation old in culture and tradition but new in ideas and concern for the welfare of its people.

This concern for people has been amply illustrated by the government's new program of self-determination for village development and by the tremendous progress that has been made in education, agriculture and other programs of direct benefit to the people. It is true that some important programs have been slow in their progress, such as the land reform movement, but in the final appraisal it must be understood that a war is in progress which complicates immeasurably the effectiveness of all programs.

Both North and South Vietnam claim to be making progress militarily in the present conflict. In July 1968, the South Vietnamese and U. S. reports claimed control of only 2000 hamlets in the rice-rich Mekong Delta and listed 2100 under Viet Cong con-

Windmills pump sea water into drying basins to produce salt.

Piles of white salt from the sea will be used to produce "Nuc Mum," the fish sauce that is used to flavor foods.

Elephants provide power to move heavy logs in the Central Highlands.

trol. By May 1971, the picture was greatly changed. The government of South Vietnam then claimed control of over 4000 hamlets in the delta, with only 14 hamlets in Viet Cong control. A gain in control of over 2000 hamlets by the South Vietnamese in the delta alone in three years can only be called progress and significant achievement.

It is doubtful, however, if the North Vietnamese and Viet Cong will agree with the above figures. My own experience with such reports while working in Vietnam has led me to be somewhat skeptical about their absolute validity. However, I do not believe that the exaggeration would be so great as to significantly change the overall military picture. I believe that South Vietnam is succeeding militarily in spite of heavy United States troop withdrawals.

The Tet offensive of 1968 in which the Viet Cong sprung a nationwide early morning attack on Tet, the Vietnamese New Year, was a decided turning point in the war. Huge losses in manpower during the Tet offensive resulted in the Viet Cong forcibly drafting men to fight for them. They were also forced to increase their pressure on the people for more taxes for more food and labor. Even the timing of the Tet offensive worked against the Viet Cong. The people were infuriated at the violation of the sanctity of such an important holiday. After Tet, new draft laws were initiated that resulted in a 50 percent increase in manpower in the South Vietnamese army.

Economic improvements in the welfare of the villages have resulted from new government programs. Awareness on the part of the rural population has increased as a result of the rapid spread of transistor radios. The lot of the rural population has improved to the extent that the urgency for change in many areas of the country is no longer present.

"The future looks promising, the present is better than it was, why fight the situation?" "The Viet Cong cannot win." "The government has its faults, but it is better than any government we had before." "Why continue to fight and die for something that may not be any better than we have now?" This seems to be the general attitude of the people.

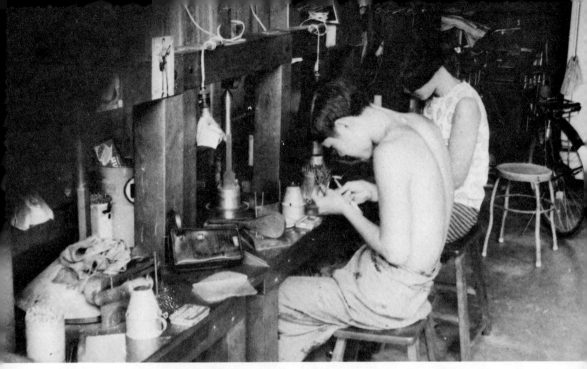
Skilled artisans cut stones for jewelry in small shops.

The little man in Vietnam, the man who really counts, wants only a few simple things from life: an education for his children so they can better themselves, his family near him, the right to worship as he pleases, and enough food on his table. If he is really lucky, he may be blessed with a piece of land of his own and a water buffalo or two. He wants more, much more, just as you and I do, but will settle for this and be content if the rest does not come.

In many cases he has fulfilled this dream and more has already arrived. His transistor radio keeps him up to date on the price of rice in Saigon. The rice merchant must now pay him a good, fair price for his rice or he will take it to Saigon himself. It is not surprising to find individual farmers going to Saigon and buying tractors for cash. Sometimes a

Clay molds, charcoal fire, old artillery shell cases and countless hours of labor with hand tools will produce beautiful brass vases, candlestick holders and bells.

group of farmers will get together and pool their money to buy a tractor. They then rent it to other farmers and soon have paid for it. When this one is paid, they buy another.

Minister of Economy Pham Kim Ngoc recently said, "The Communists are handicapped. They don't understand profits — the incentive of the market economy. They are more concerned with making men ideological believers than materially happy. Therefore, they sanctify poverty.

"Our attitude is: Let us put chickens in the hands of the farmer. Then he has something to defend."*

In keeping with this philosophy, the government has redistributed old French lands to peasant farmers. In addition, they have purchased 2.5 million acres from landlords and distributed them free to 800,000 tenant farmers. Many of the others are able to secure long-term, low-interest loans to purchase improved rice seed and fertilizer. All this gives farmers an ownership stake in the system of government, something they didn't have before. Now they are one of the landowners the Viet Cong has been persecuting. A system of government ownership of the land, as found under communism, no longer has much appeal to the new landowner. His patriotism and loyalty to the government of South Vietnam increases considerably.

---

*J. A. Livingston, "Viet Boom Likened to Indonesia," *Business Outlook, The Minneapolis Star*, Tues., July 20, 1971.

Hand looms compete with large mills to produce textiles.

Vietnamese are learning about new ways of working together. Labor unions and cooperatives are organizing throughout the country. In the village of Tuy Phong, John Lewellan, a young American I.V.S. (International Voluntary Service) volunteer, encouraged a group of Vietnamese to pool their resources and form an electrical cooperative. After many months of scrounging and hard work, John was able to report the successful electrification of a village of 25,000 people through the efforts of members of their own community. Community development of this type is taking place throughout Vietnam.

The new IR-8 rice from the Philippines, the use of commercial fertilizer and improved farming meth-

Newly dyed cloth produced in a riverside home hangs in the sun to dry.

ods have resulted in yields that frequently are up to four times the amount that was formerly produced on the same field. In 1967, more than 700,000 metric tons of rice were imported into South Vietnam. In 1969, only half that amount was imported, and the 1971 crop reduced this amount to 138,000 tons. Vietnam will soon be supplying rice to other countries of Southeast Asia.

Fish production has, through the use of nylon nets and motorized boats, increased from 165,000 tons in 1959 to more than 600,000 tons in 1971. Vietnam now exports fish to other countries.

Before the country was divided, almost all industry was in the North. By the end of 1967, South Vietnam had in operation more than 800 new factories—textile, cement, pharmaceutical, plastic, paint—employing 75,000 workers and contributing a quarter of the gross national product.

Perhaps the greatest need facing Vietnam is the need for trained, capable leaders. This need is being met through massive programs such as the development and training of hundreds of thousands of Revolutionary Development Cadre. This program involves training villagers in basic skills in education, agriculture, sanitation and other relevant fields as well as in military defense and returning them to the villages to help with the problems of the villagers. This program has met with both failure and success in aiding the welfare of villagers, but certainly has been successful in extending new knowledge and skill to thousands.

Massive programs in vocational training, education, agriculture, fishery technology and village administration are also under way.

Thousands of village officials have completed training courses in all aspects of village management and are thereby better able to meet the needs of the people.

In Binh Thuan province alone, 586 village and hamlet officials attended five-week courses in taxation, planning, registration of marriages, births and deaths, and in the many skills necessary in their positions.

Potter's wheels in skilled hands turn clay into beauty.

A foot-powered lathe helps smooth the surface of a lacquerware bowl.

Imported automobiles, souvenir jackets and Buddhist monks.

Refugees are being trained in new skills and are given land for farming to aid in creating a new life. The enormity of the job has resulted in slow progress in this direction, but the plan is in effect, the funds are available and time should see the accomplishment of the stated goals.

For the first time in the history of Vietnam free elections are being held and the people have a true voice in the choice of their leaders. Cries of intrigue, political maneuvering and unfair elections are heard in the capitals of the world. My own personal observation of the village elections in Binh Thuan province in 1968 led me to believe that the elections were fairly run and did represent the wishes of the people. Ninety-six percent of the eligible voters turned out and voted in the elections. Most positions offered a choice of from three to fifteen candidates.

I could not help but admire a man who sought election as a village or hamlet official, a job with no pay, only hard work, and the constant threat of assassination by the Viet Cong. Since 1954, thousands of officials, teachers, and potential leaders have been systematically annihilated, creating a real shortage of capable, trained leadership. Hardly a week passed in Binh Thuan province without the assassination, sometimes in broad daylight on crowded streets, of one or more elected officials. Yet in spite of the danger and personal sacrifice, every public office had several men seeking election. This, in my opinion, is the utmost in devotion to people and one's country.

A nation composed of men such as these cannot help but succeed.

When I arrived in Binh Thuan province in 1967, 40,000 tons of rice a year were being imported to feed the people. When I left in 1969, rice production had been so improved by newer methods and the introduction of IR-8 rice from the Philippines that it was not necessary to import rice. For the first time since the 1920s Binh Thuan was again raising enough rice to feed its people. The price of rice is stabilizing

Vietnamese soldiers use modern weapons.

and the rate of inflation is declining. This is the kind of progress that means the most to the people.

Of the 5,000 or more fishing boats in the province, over half had recently installed gasoline-operated motors that enabled them to go farther and catch more fish. Almost all the fishermen were using the new nylon nets that required less care and also caught more fish. The overall production of the fishing industry had been greatly increased. Fishermen were prospering. Even fishermen in some of the refugee camps were able to build new homes of brick and send their children to school.

174

Junior Chamber International, Rotary, Lions, Knights of Columbus and other worldwide organizations find new members in Vietnam who are eager to learn about community development and leadership training.

What the future holds for Vietnam is difficult to predict. It is certain, however, that if present programs are allowed to continue, the people will prosper and continue to improve their way of life.

Vietnam is a country rich in potential for providing food for its people and those of other Asian nations. Agriculture and fishing offer the greatest opportunity for future development.

Small quantities of tin, limestone and coal are available to form the basis of a limited industrialization.

175

Old friends bid farewell.

Peace and Progress—a dream or a reality?

The huge rubber plantations are presently limited in their production and must compete not only with the hostilities of the war, but also with the decreasing demand for natural rubber brought on by extensive use of synthetics. Rubber will undoubtedly continue to be an important product, but will in all likelihood not form the basis for a new economic base.

Rumors of off-shore oil are only rumors. Time alone will tell of the potential in this area.

The wealth of Vietnam lies essentially in the land and in the people.

In the event that a stable government unburdened by the tribulations of a wartime economy should come to Vietnam, I have no doubt that the people of this new nation will rise to meet the challenge and become an important asset to the world's economy.

The unquenchable spirit of the people has survived through centuries of outside domination and internal strife. They will continue to be a gracious, hard-working, industrious people filled with pride in their heritage and love of their land, undaunted by the trials of life, looking constantly ahead to a better tomorrow through their own diligent effort.

BIBLIOGRAPHY

BOOKS

Dareff, Hal. *The Story of Vietnam.* (n.p.): Parents Magazine Press, 1966.

Devillers, Philippe. *Histoire du Vietnam.* Paris: Editions du Sevil, 1952.

Fall, Bernard. *The Two Viet-Nams.* New York: Frederick A. Praeger, Inc., 1964.

Hammer, Ellen. *Vietnam—Yesterday and Today.* New York: Holt, Rinehart and Winston, Inc., 1966.

Isaacs, Harold. *No Peace for Asia.* New York: Macmillan, 1947.

Kahlin, George McTurnan, and John W. Lewis. *The United States in Vietnam.* (n.p.): Dial Press, Inc., 1967.

Reischauer, Edwin O., and John K. Fairbank. *East Asia The Great Tradition.* Boston: Houghton Mifflin Company, 1958.

Shamsulhuq, Muhammad. *Education and Development Strategy in South and Southeast Asia.* Kingsport, Tennessee: Kingsport Press, Inc., 1965.

Sun, Ruth Q. (ed.). *Land of Sea Gull and Fox— Folk Tales of Vietnam.* Tokyo: John Weatherhill, Inc., 1966.

Thompson, Sir Robert. *Defeating Communist Insurgency—The Lessons of Malaya and Vietnam.* New York: Frederick A. Praeger, Inc., 1966.

GOVERNMENT PUBLICATIONS

An Introduction to Vietnam, Second Edition. The Vietnam Council of Foreign Relations, Saigon: Saigon An-Quan, Inc., 1969.

Annuaire Statistique de L'Enseignement, 1965-1966, Vietnam. Republique Du Vietnam, Ministere De L'Education De La Culture De La Jeunesse.

Harris, George L., *et al. U.S. Army Area Handbook for Vietnam.* Washington: Government Printing Office, 1964.

Progress of Education In Vietnam During the School Year 1966-1967. Republic of Vietnam, Ministry of Education. Geneva: XXXth International Conference on Public Education, July 1967.

Student Records From Vietnam. Prepared by The Education Division, United States Operations Mission to Vietnam, Revised February, 1964.

Tha-Duc, Demonstration Secondary School. Republic of Vietnam, Ministry of Culture, Education and Youth, University of Saigon, Faculty of Pedagogy.

USARV (United States Army Vietnam) *Fact Sheet,* Issue No. 22-68. San Francisco: Information Office, USARV, June 2, 1968.

Vietnam Teacher Education Project. Study Tour for
   1967.
Current Foreign Policy. U.S. Assistance Program in
   Viet-Nam Department of State. Washington: U.S.
   Government Printing Office, Revised July 1972.

PERIODICALS

"After the War: A Bonanza for South Vietnam,"
   U.S. News and World Report, January 19, 1970,
   p. 34.
"Ahead—Faster Withdrawal From Vietnam," Re-
   sults of Laird Mission, *U.S. News and World Re-
   port,* February 23, 1970, p. 29.
Sevareid, Eric. "Why Our Foreign Policy Is Failing,"
   Look, May 3, 1966, pp. 25-26.
Tanham, George K. "Nationalism and Revolution,"
   Asia, No. 4, Winter, 1966.
"Vietnam, A Special Issue," *Asian Survey,* Vol. VII,
   No. 8, August, 1967. Berkeley, California: The
   Institute of International Studies, University of
   California.
"Why We Didn't Win In Vietnam," *U.S. News and
   World Report,* January 19, 1970, p. 34.

UNPUBLISHED MATERIALS

"A Summary History of Vietnam," A pamphlet with
   source given as "unknown."
"1968-69 Annual Report," Government of Vietnam,
   Ministry of Education, Saigon, Vietnam.

"An Introduction to the General Use of the New Ministry Textbooks," The Ministry of Education Textbook Program, October, 1967. Taken from lecture notes by Ann M. Domidion, presented at the 1968 teacher training session in Binh Thuan Province, Vietnam.

"Briefing Materials," Office of Education, USAID/ Vietnam, 1969.

"Education in Region II," New Life Development Division, Education Branch, Civil Operations and Revolutionary Development Support, II Corps, Nha Trang, July, 1968.

"Education Vietnam: Proposal for Reorganization," Report of the National Education Study Team, Wisconsin State University—Stevens Point.

"Five Year Education Plan 1966-1970," Republic of Vietnam, Ministry of Education.

"Form—VN/ED 12-10-68," Government of Vietnam, Ministry of Education.

"Report on Educational Developments in 1967-1968," Republic of Vietnam, Ministry of Culture, Education and Youth.

"Secondary Education (690-365)," 1968-1969 C.A.P. Presentation, USAID Office of Education, Saigon, Vietnam.

Trai, Nguyen. "Pacification of the Ngo," Taken from a pamphlet with no source or publisher given.

NEWSPAPERS

New York Times, June 28, 1964.

OTHER REFERENCES

An interview with Mr. Loan, Education Chief, Ministry of Education, Phan Thiet, Binh Thuan Province, Vietnam.

Nguyen-Van-Thai, and Nguyen-Van-Mung. "A Short History of Vietnam," Publishd for the Vietnamese-American Association, Saigon, Vietnam: The Times Publishing Company, 1958, 8 pp.

INDEX